Using AI in Academic Writing and Research

Eldar Haber • Dariusz Jemielniak
Artur Kurasiński • Aleksandra Przegalińska

Using AI in Academic Writing and Research

A Complete Guide to Effective and Ethical
Academic AI

Eldar Haber
Faculty of Law, University of Haifa
Haifa, Israel

Dariusz Jemielniak
Kozminski University
Warszawa, Poland

Artur Kurasiński
Warszawa, Poland

Aleksandra Przegalińska
Kozminski University
Warszawa, Poland

ISBN 978-3-031-91704-2   ISBN 978-3-031-91705-9   (eBook)
https://doi.org/10.1007/978-3-031-91705-9

This Palgrave Macmillan imprint is published by the registered company Springer Nature Switzerland AG.
The registered company address is: Gewerbestrasse 11, 6330 Cham, Switzerland

If disposing of this product, please recycle the paper.   ·

CONTENTS

List of Practical Examples

CHAPTER 1

Introduction: Generative AI in Academia—A Transformative Frontier

Abstract The introduction sets the stage for a critical and practical examination of generative AI's role in academia. It argues that tools like GPT, Claude, Gemini, and Llama are not merely automating academic tasks but transforming the nature of research, writing, teaching, and institutional practice. By mapping the historical trajectory of AI—from symbolic logic to large language models—it underscores the significance of the generative turn and its implications for knowledge production. The chapter outlines the book's goals: to provide researchers, educators, and academic administrators with a balanced, accessible, and research-informed framework for engaging with AI responsibly. Foundational concepts, model architectures, and the mechanics of language generation are introduced to equip readers with a technical and historical understanding of the tools reshaping scholarly work.

Keywords Generative AI • Academic research • Large language models • AI ethics • Higher education

Artificial Intelligence is no longer a distant theoretical concept—it is actively reshaping academic work. The emergence of generative AI, particularly large language models (LLMs) such as OpenAI's GPT, Anthropic's Claude, Meta's Llama, and Google's Gemini, has introduced new ways of

© The Author(s), under exclusive license to Springer Nature Switzerland AG 2025
E. Haber et al., *Using AI in Academic Writing and Research*,
https://doi.org/10.1007/978-3-031-91705-9_1

conducting research, generating content, analyzing data, and even engaging with students. As these technologies continue to evolve, they are not just tools for automation but catalysts for transformation, influencing scholarly thinking, institutional practices, and ethical debates.

This book examines generative AI's transformative potential in academia, offering practical insights into its applications, mechanics, and broader implications. By analyzing current AI implementation and anticipating future developments, we equip scholars, educators, and administrators with essential knowledge to navigate—and thrive within—this rapidly evolving landscape.

Purpose and Scope

The primary goal of this book is to provide a structured, research-informed perspective on generative AI's role in academia. We go beyond simplistic narratives of AI as either a utopian solution or an existential threat. Instead, we explore the nuanced realities of integrating AI into research, writing, data management, teaching, and academic governance.

To achieve this, we present a comprehensive roadmap covering:

- **The Evolution of AI**: A historical overview of artificial intelligence, from early symbolic models to the deep learning revolution that enabled today's generative AI (Chap. 2).
- **AI for Research**: How generative AI assists in literature reviews, hypothesis generation, and conceptual development, while also raising concerns about bias and intellectual integrity (Chap. 3).
- **Writing and Publishing**: The role of AI in drafting research papers, structuring arguments, and streamlining the academic publication process (Chap. 4).
- **Data Management and Analysis**: The integration of AI in structuring, cleaning, and interpreting large datasets, reducing manual workloads and enabling new forms of discovery (Chap. 5).
- **Presentation and Dissemination**: How AI enhances academic presentations, public engagement, and the visualization of complex research findings (Chap. 6).
- **Future Trends**: Speculative but evidence-based insights into how AI might continue to shape academia in the coming years (Chap. 7).
- **Practical Tips and Resources**: Guidance on leveraging AI effectively while maintaining scholarly rigor and critical thinking (Chap. 8).

- **Regulatory and Ethical Challenges**: The legal, ethical, and institutional debates surrounding AI use in academic work, including issues of authorship, data privacy, and misinformation (Chap. 9).

This book is designed for a broad academic audience, including:

- **Researchers** looking to integrate AI into their workflows, from literature synthesis to data analysis.
- **Educators** seeking innovative ways to enhance student engagement and optimize instructional materials.
- **Graduate students** navigating the dual challenge of mastering AI-assisted research while developing their own critical perspectives.
- **Administrators and policymakers** who need to understand the institutional implications of AI adoption in higher education.

While AI literacy is not a prerequisite for engaging with this book, we provide foundational explanations of key concepts to ensure accessibility across disciplines. Each chapter of this book delves into specific areas where AI is making an impact. From assisting in research ideation to managing large-scale data, AI is proving to be a valuable collaborator in academia. However, its use also raises critical concerns—particularly regarding transparency, intellectual property, and the potential deskilling of researchers.

We offer a balanced perspective on its benefits and limitations by highlighting practical case studies and providing hands-on strategies for integrating AI into scholarly work. This includes:

- How AI can enhance, but not replace, rigorous academic writing.
- The role of AI in data processing and visualization, particularly in handling large, unstructured datasets.
- Ethical guidelines for using AI responsibly, ensuring that it complements rather than compromises academic integrity.

FOUNDATIONAL CONCEPTS: UNDERSTANDING GENERATIVE AI

To effectively engage with generative AI, it is crucial to understand how these systems work, what their limitations are, and how they differ from other types of artificial intelligence. AI in academia is often discussed in broad terms, but generative AI refers specifically to models capable of producing human-like text, images, code, and even music. This section breaks down the key components of generative AI, including how it is trained, the core models used today, and the theoretical underpinnings that drive its capabilities.

Generative AI is a subset of artificial intelligence specializing in creating new content rather than simply classifying, analyzing, or retrieving existing information. Unlike traditional AI models designed for specific tasks—such as spam detection, image recognition, or recommendation systems—generative AI can generate novel outputs based on learned patterns. It uses probabilistic methods, predicting the most likely sequence of words, pixels, or sound waves to create coherent and contextually relevant content.

Modern generative AI is primarily driven by deep learning, a branch of machine learning that utilizes multi-layered artificial neural networks. These networks process vast amounts of data to identify relationships, structures, and contextual nuances that allow them to mimic human-generated content. However, it is essential to emphasize that AI does not "understand" as humans do. Instead, it operates based on statistical correlations, mapping input to likely output without possessing intrinsic knowledge, reasoning, or intentionality.

Key Models and Architectures: The Brains Behind Generative AI

Several major AI models have emerged as dominant forces in generative AI, each with distinct architectures and applications. Understanding these models helps demystify how AI-generated content is created and where its strengths and limitations lie.

1. Transformer-Based Models: The Backbone of Modern AI

The breakthrough that enabled today's generative AI was the introduction of the **transformer architecture**. Unlike earlier neural network models that processed input sequentially (such as recurrent neural networks, RNNs), transformers use **self-attention mechanisms** to analyze entire input sequences in parallel. This allows models to recognize long-range dependencies in text, significantly improving their ability to generate coherent, context-aware responses.

The most widely used transformer-based models include:

- **GPT (Generative Pre-trained Transformer)**—Developed by OpenAI, this family of models (GPT-3, GPT-4, and future versions) is trained on massive text corpora to generate fluent, human-like text. GPT models are widely used in academic writing, coding, and conversational AI.
- **Claude**—Created by Anthropic, Claude focuses on safety, interpretability, and reduced bias, making it a strong alternative for responsible AI use in academia.
- **BERT (Bidirectional Encoder Representations from Transformers)**—Unlike GPT, which is generative, BERT is primarily designed for understanding and classifying text. It excels in tasks such as question answering and text summarization.
- **Gemini (Google's AI suite, formerly Bard)**—A multimodal AI that integrates textual, visual, and auditory data to enhance generative AI's adaptability.
- **Llama (Meta's Large Language Model Meta AI)**—A high-performance, open-source alternative to proprietary models, designed for customization and scalability.
- **DeepSeek**—A highly efficient, open-source Chinese alternative to proprietary models, using the so-called multi-head latent attention to reduce the size of the key-value cache, allowing for much less resource-intensive queries.

All these models share the transformer-based structure, but their training objectives differ. GPT models generate text in an autoregressive fashion (predicting the next word based on prior context). In contrast, BERT is optimized for bidirectional understanding, making it better suited for language comprehension tasks rather than text generation.

2. Training Generative AI: From Raw Data to Intelligent Outputs

Generative AI models are trained in three key phases:

1. **Pre-training**—Models are exposed to enormous datasets (e.g., books, academic articles, Wikipedia, and internet forums) to learn general linguistic patterns, syntax, and factual associations. During this phase, they predict missing words in sentences, refining their ability to generate coherent language.

2. **Fine-tuning**—After pre-training, models undergo refinement with targeted datasets, ensuring alignment with specific use cases. For example, an AI model fine-tuned for academic writing may be trained on journal articles and conference proceedings to improve domain-specific accuracy.
3. **Reinforcement Learning from Human Feedback (RLHF)**—This process enhances AI's performance by incorporating human judgments on generated responses. Trainers rank AI-generated outputs, reinforcing desirable behaviors such as factual accuracy, coherence, and ethical considerations.

Even with these training steps, generative AI models remain **stochastic**—their outputs are probabilistic rather than deterministic. This means that the same prompt can yield different responses each time, making AI-generated content useful for ideation but unreliable for factual consistency without human oversight.

How AI "Thinks": The Mechanics of Language Generation

A common misconception is that AI generates text by retrieving pre-written responses. In reality, LLMs do not "cut/copy-paste" from their training data, but instead generate text dynamically based on probability distributions. Here's how the process works:

1. **Tokenization**—Text is broken down into smaller units called **tokens**, which can be words, subwords, or even characters. For instance, the phrase "machine learning" might be split into ["machine," "learning"] or ["mach," "ine," "learning"] depending on the tokenizer used.
2. **Contextual Analysis**—Using self-attention, the model determines which words in a sequence are most relevant to predicting the next token.
3. **Next-Token Prediction**—The AI selects the most statistically probable next word based on its training data and the given input. If there is ambiguity, it generates an output based on **temperature settings** (a parameter controlling randomness—lower values yield deterministic answers, while higher values encourage creative variation).

4. **Iteration and Completion**—The process repeats until the model reaches a predefined stopping point (such as a sentence or paragraph limit).

This method explains why AI-generated text can sometimes be overconfidently wrong—it does not verify facts but rather constructs plausible-sounding sequences based on prior patterns.

HISTORICAL CONTEXT: FROM SYMBOLIC AI TO THE GENERATIVE REVOLUTION

The field of artificial intelligence has experienced dramatic shifts over the past several decades, moving through cycles of intense optimism, funding booms, setbacks, and resurgence. The rise of generative AI represents the latest transformation in this ongoing evolution, but its foundations were laid by earlier breakthroughs in symbolic reasoning, machine learning, and neural networks. Understanding this history is essential to appreciating both the current moment and the trajectory AI is likely to follow in academia and beyond.

The origins of artificial intelligence can be traced back to the 1950s, when researchers sought to create machines capable of replicating human reasoning. Alan Turing's seminal paper *"Computing Machinery and Intelligence"* (1950) posed the question, *"Can machines think?"*, and introduced the now-famous Turing Test as a benchmark for artificial intelligence. Around the same time, John McCarthy, Marvin Minsky, Herbert Simon, and Allen Newell developed early AI programs that performed symbolic reasoning, solving logic puzzles and proving mathematical theorems.

- The Logic Theorist (1956) and General Problem Solver (1957) by Newell and Simon aimed to automate logical reasoning.
- McCarthy coined the term Artificial Intelligence in 1956 at the Dartmouth Conference, the field's founding event.
- Early natural language processing (NLP) systems, such as ELIZA (1966) by Joseph Weizenbaum, attempted to simulate human conversation.

During this era, AI research was dominated by symbolic approaches, which involved explicitly programmed rules for problem-solving. However, these early systems struggled with real-world complexity—they worked well in constrained environments (such as chess playing) but failed in open-ended tasks requiring common-sense reasoning.

The first "AI Winter" (1973–1980s) was triggered by growing skepticism over AI's grand promises and practical limitations. Two critical reports fueled this skepticism:

1. The Lighthill Report (1973) in the UK argued that AI had failed to achieve its ambitious goals and was unlikely to justify continued government funding.
2. DARPA (U.S. Defense Advanced Research Projects Agency) also scaled back funding, concluding that AI research was producing diminishing returns.

As a result, many AI projects lost funding, and research slowed. The main challenges were:

- Computational limitations: Early AI models required immense processing power that was unavailable at the time.
- Lack of adaptability: AI systems could not generalize knowledge outside narrow, predefined rules.
- Failures of symbolic AI: Rule-based systems could not handle ambiguous, probabilistic, or incomplete data.

Despite this downturn, seeds of the future AI resurgence were quietly being sown. Researchers in the late 1980s began shifting their focus from symbolic AI toward connectionist models, which later formed the foundation for deep learning.

By the 1990s, advances in computational power, statistical modeling, and data availability led to a revival of AI research, marking the transition from rule-based AI to data-driven approaches.

- Machine learning emerged as the dominant paradigm, shifting AI systems from explicitly programmed rules to learning from data.
- Support Vector Machines (SVMs) and Hidden Markov Models (HMMs) made pattern recognition and speech processing breakthroughs.

- Neural networks were revived thanks to improved training algorithms, such as backpropagation (Hinton, 1986).

This shift enabled practical applications like spam filtering, recommendation systems, and early voice assistants (e.g., IBM's Watson). AI began moving out of the research lab and into real-world applications.

The 2010s saw an explosion in AI capabilities, driven by three key factors:

1. Unprecedented computational power—The advent of Graphics Processing Units (GPUs), originally designed for gaming, enabled large-scale neural network training.
2. Big Data availability—The internet, social media, and digitized academic resources provided AI with vast datasets to learn from.
3. Breakthrough algorithms—Developing deep neural networks, particularly Convolutional Neural Networks (CNNs) for image recognition and Recurrent Neural Networks (RNNs) for language modeling, transformed the field.

Some key milestones include:

- 2012—The AlexNet model won the ImageNet competition, proving the power of deep learning for visual recognition.
- 2014—The invention of Generative Adversarial Networks (GANs) (Goodfellow et al.), enabling AI to generate realistic images, deepfakes, and artistic content.
- 2017—The introduction of transformer models (*"Attention Is All You Need,"* Vaswani et al.), which paved the way for large language models like GPT.

With the advent of transformer-based architectures, generative AI entered a new phase of sophistication. Unlike earlier models that classified or predicted based on pre-existing patterns, these new systems could generate coherent, original text, code, images, and even synthetic voices.

Key developments in LLMs (Large Language Models) include:

- GPT-3 (2020)—A landmark in AI-generated text, capable of sophisticated responses and creative writing.

- DALL·E (2021)—A model generating AI-created images from text prompts, marking a leap in multimodal AI.
- ChatGPT (2022)—Brought generative AI into mainstream use, revolutionizing human-AI interaction.
- Claude, Llama, and Gemini (2023–2024)—Competing AI models offering advancements in reasoning, contextual coherence, and ethical safeguards.
- DeepSeek (2025)—A model bringing significant efficiency gains, questioning the need for expensive hardware to achieve top results.

The history of AI reveals recurring cycles of hype and disillusionment. While today's AI capabilities are undeniably transformative, there are enduring risks:

- Overpromising vs. reality—The AI Winters of the past teach us that inflated expectations can lead to backlash when AI fails to deliver on grandiose claims.
- Human-AI collaboration—AI does not replace researchers; it enhances their ability to work efficiently, think critically, and engage with complex ideas.
- Ethical and regulatory awareness—The rapid evolution of AI necessitates ongoing discussions about responsible use, transparency, and governance.

The Path Ahead

As we move forward, generative AI will continue profoundly shaping academic work. The challenge for scholars, educators, and institutions is not whether to use AI but how to use it responsibly. This book provides a historically informed, critically engaged exploration of AI's potential in academia, ensuring that its integration aligns with scholarly values, ethical considerations, and intellectual rigor.

Rather than viewing AI as a neutral tool, we encourage academics to engage with these technologies critically. AI is not simply an efficiency booster but a force shaping the nature of knowledge production and dissemination. By understanding its mechanics, leveraging its strengths, and mitigating its weaknesses, scholars can harness AI's potential while maintaining the integrity of academic inquiry.

This book does not offer a one-size-fits-all prescription for AI use in academia. Instead, it provides a foundation for informed decision-making, equipping readers with the knowledge and strategies needed to navigate this rapidly changing field. As we embark on this journey through AI's role in academia, we invite readers to approach it with curiosity, caution, and a commitment to ethical scholarship.

CHAPTER 2

The Evolution of Artificial Intelligence: From Winter to Renaissance

Abstract This chapter traces the historical trajectory of artificial intelligence, from its symbolic beginnings and early optimism through the disillusionment of the AI Winter, to the current renaissance powered by deep learning and transformer-based models. It examines the factors that enabled AI's resurgence—advances in computational power, data availability, and algorithmic innovation—and culminates in the rise of generative AI as a paradigm-shifting development. The chapter also critically assesses ongoing challenges, including environmental costs, infrastructure limitations, data scarcity, and equity concerns. By anchoring contemporary breakthroughs in historical perspective, it underscores the need for balanced, responsible innovation that avoids the overpromising that once stalled the field's progress.

Keywords AI Winter • Deep learning • Neural networks • Generative AI • Transformer models • Computational power • Data-driven AI • Responsible innovation

THE AI WINTER: A HISTORICAL PERSPECTIVE

The story of artificial intelligence is one of dramatic peaks and valleys, with perhaps no valley deeper than the period known as the "AI Winter" (Hendler, 2008). The field's inception can be traced to a watershed

E. Haber et al., *Using AI in Academic Writing and Research*, https://doi.org/10.1007/978-3-031-91705-9_2

moment in 1956 at the Dartmouth Summer Research Project, where John McCarthy coined the term "artificial intelligence" (McCarthy et al., 1955). This gathering of brilliant minds, including Marvin Minsky, Claude Shannon, and Herbert Simon, marked the beginning of AI as a formal discipline.

The foundations for this new field had been laid earlier by Alan Turing's seminal paper "Computing Machinery and Intelligence" (1950), which introduced the famous Turing Test and established fundamental concepts about machine intelligence. These early pioneers envisioned machines that could replicate human cognitive abilities, from problem-solving to natural language understanding (McCorduck, 2004).

The 1950s and early 1960s witnessed remarkable initial successes. Newell and Simon's Logic Theorist (1956) became the first program to prove mathematical theorems, while their General Problem Solver (GPS) demonstrated basic reasoning capabilities (Newell et al., 1959). These achievements, coupled with advances in natural language processing like Weizenbaum's ELIZA (1966), created a wave of optimism. The period saw substantial funding from both government agencies, particularly DARPA's Information Processing Techniques Office (IPTO), and corporate research laboratories like MIT's AI Lab and Stanford's AI Laboratory (Roland & Shiman, 2002).

However, the field's ambitious goals soon encountered significant obstacles. The limitations of symbolic AI—the dominant paradigm of the time—became increasingly apparent. These systems, based on formal logic and rule-based reasoning, struggled with real-world complexity, particularly in areas requiring common-sense reasoning or pattern recognition (Dreyfus, 1972; Deng et al., 2009; Dong & Srivastava, 2013; Boden, 2016; Dennett, 2017; Floridi, 2019). The "microworld" approach, exemplified by Winograd's SHRDLU program, while successful in constrained environments, failed to scale to more complex, real-world scenarios (Winograd, 1972).

By the mid-1970s, mounting criticism culminated in several devastating reports. The Lighthill Report (1973), commissioned by the British Science Research Council, particularly criticized AI's failure to achieve its "grandiose objectives" and questioned the field's practical value. The report's impact was immediate and severe, leading to the virtual elimination of AI research funding in Britain (Lighthill, 1973). Similar skepticism spread through the United States, as DARPA and other major funders grew disillusioned with AI's progress (Crevier, 1993).

The ensuing AI Winter of the 1970s and 1980s was characterized by a cascade of setbacks. The collapse of the commercial market for AI systems, particularly expert systems, led to the dissolution of many AI companies and research programs. XCON, developed by Digital Equipment Corporation, exemplified these challenges—while initially successful, its maintenance costs spiraled as the system grew more complex (McDermott, 1982). The limitations of expert systems became clear: they were brittle, unable to learn from experience, and required extensive manual knowledge engineering.

This period of retrenchment, while painful, proved invaluable for the field's development. It fostered a more rigorous approach to AI research, emphasizing empirical evaluation and realistic goal-setting. The winter years also saw the quiet emergence of approaches that would later revolutionize the field, particularly in neural networks and probabilistic reasoning (Nilsson, 2009). The connection machine, developed by Danny Hillis in the 1980s, represented early attempts at parallel processing architectures that would later prove crucial for deep learning (Hillis, 1985).

The AI Winter taught the field critical lessons about the dangers of over-promising and the importance of managing expectations. It demonstrated that progress in AI requires not just algorithmic innovations but also advances in computational infrastructure and theoretical understanding. Perhaps most importantly, it highlighted the need for a more nuanced appreciation of intelligence itself—recognition that human cognition is far more complex than initially assumed, requiring multiple approaches and sustained, incremental progress rather than quick breakthroughs (Brooks, 1991).

THE RESURGENCE OF AI: FACTORS ENABLING THE CURRENT BOOM

The thaw in AI development began gradually in the late 1990s and early 2000s, driven by several concurrent technological and infrastructural developments. The most significant breakthrough came with the revival of neural networks through deep learning, a resurgence that would fundamentally transform the field. This renaissance was enabled by three crucial factors that converged to create the perfect storm for AI advancement: unprecedented computational power, massive data availability, and revolutionary algorithmic innovations (Goodfellow et al., 2016).

The Computational Revolution: GPUs and Beyond

The rise of Graphics Processing Units (GPUs) marked a transformative moment in the computational landscape. Originally engineered for rendering complex 3D graphics in video games, these processors possessed a unique architecture that proved serendipitously ideal for the parallel processing demands of neural networks. Unlike traditional Central Processing Units (CPUs) designed for sequential processing, GPUs could perform thousands of simultaneous calculations—a capability perfectly aligned with the matrix operations fundamental to neural network training (Oh & Jung, 2004).

NVIDIA's introduction of CUDA (Compute Unified Device Architecture) in 2006 represented a pivotal moment, providing developers direct access to GPU's parallel compute capabilities (NVIDIA, 2018). This development transformed GPUs from specialized gaming hardware into general-purpose computing powerhouses. The company subsequently recognized the emerging potential for AI applications and began developing specialized architectures. The release of the Tesla architecture in 2007, followed by successive generations of AI-optimized hardware, dramatically accelerated training times and enabled the development of increasingly complex models (Kirk & Hwu, 2017).

The impact was profound: tasks that once required weeks of computation could now be completed in days or hours. For instance, the training of AlexNet in 2012—a watershed moment for deep learning—leveraged two NVIDIA GTX 580 GPUs to achieve breakthrough performance in image recognition, reducing training time from weeks to days (Krizhevsky et al., 2012).

The Data Revolution: From Scarcity to Abundance

The digital revolution provided another crucial ingredient: an unprecedented abundance of data. The explosive growth of the internet, proliferation of social media platforms, and widespread digitization of industries created vast datasets suitable for training AI systems. This data revolution was characterized by transformative developments in multiple domains. The emergence of social media platforms generated massive amounts of user-generated content, providing natural language data at an unprecedented scale. Concurrent with this development, the widespread adoption of mobile devices with sophisticated sensors created rich datasets of images, location data, and user interactions. The nascent Internet of Things (IoT) began producing continuous streams of sensor data from millions of connected devices, while digital transformation initiatives across industries generated structured datasets from healthcare, finance, and industrial processes.

Cloud computing platforms emerged as a democratizing force, fundamentally changing how researchers and organizations could access and process these massive datasets. Services like Amazon Web Services (AWS), Google Cloud Platform, and Microsoft Azure eliminated the need for massive upfront infrastructure investments. This democratization enabled startups and researchers to experiment with AI at scales previously reserved for large tech companies (Jonas et al., 2019).

Algorithmic Breakthroughs: From Theory to Practice

The convergence of computational and data advantages combined synergistically with theoretical breakthroughs in machine learning algorithms. In the domain of architectural innovations, the refinement of backpropagation techniques made training deep neural networks more practical, while the development of convolutional neural networks (CNNs) revolutionized computer vision tasks. Concurrently, Recurrent Neural Networks (RNNs) and Long Short-Term Memory (LSTM) networks enabled better processing of sequential data, complemented by the introduction of dropout and batch normalization techniques that addressed key training challenges (Hochreiter & Schmidhuber, 1997; He et al., 2016; Jouppi et al., 2017).

Significant advances in optimization techniques further accelerated progress in the field. The development of improved optimization algorithms like Adam provided faster and more stable training, while better initialization techniques helped address the vanishing gradient problem. The introduction of new activation functions, particularly the Rectified Linear Unit (ReLU), enabled faster training and better performance across a wide range of applications.

Understanding of training dynamics also improved substantially during this period. Researchers developed deeper insights into loss landscapes, leading to optimized network architectures. Advanced regularization techniques reduced overfitting, while the development of transfer learning approaches enabled more efficient use of pre-trained models. This enhanced theoretical understanding facilitated the creation of more robust and efficient neural network architectures.

The synergy between these three pillars—computation, data, and algorithms—created a powerful feedback loop. More powerful hardware enabled larger models and datasets, which drove algorithmic improvements, which in turn spurred hardware optimizations. This virtuous cycle continues to accelerate AI development today, leading to increasingly sophisticated models and applications (LeCun et al., 2015).

The Rise of Generative AI: A Paradigm Shift

The emergence of generative AI marks a transformative chapter in artificial intelligence, built upon several groundbreaking innovations in deep learning architecture and training methodologies. This shift began with the introduction of transformer architectures in 2017, which fundamentally revolutionized how AI systems process sequential data (Sejnowski, 2018; Russell & Norvig, 2020). The key innovation of attention mechanisms—allowing models to weigh the importance of different input elements dynamically—proved remarkably effective across various domains, surpassing previous approaches in both efficiency and capability (Vaswani et al., 2017).

The transformer architecture introduced several crucial innovations in neural network design. The self-attention mechanism enabled direct modeling of relationships between all elements in a sequence, regardless of their distance, effectively addressing the long-range dependency problems that had plagued earlier architectures. The multi-head attention mechanism further enhanced this capability by allowing models to capture different types of relationships simultaneously. These architectural innovations were complemented by positional encodings, which preserved sequence order information while enabling parallel processing (Devlin et al., 2019).

Large Language Models (LLMs) emerged as the first major success story of transformer-based architectures, demonstrating unprecedented capabilities in natural language processing. The progression from the original GPT (Generative Pre-trained Transformer) through successive generations illustrated the remarkable scalability of the transformer architecture. Each iteration brought significant improvements in language understanding and generation capabilities, with models exhibiting increasingly sophisticated behaviors such as in-context learning and task generalization. The scaling laws discovered during this period revealed a systematic relationship between model size, training data volume, and performance, suggesting that larger models, trained on more extensive datasets, could achieve qualitatively different capabilities (Kaplan et al., 2020).

The development of BERT (Bidirectional Encoder Representations from Transformers) introduced bidirectional context understanding, enabling more nuanced comprehension of language structure and meaning. This innovation spawned numerous architectural variants optimized for specific applications, from RoBERTa's robust optimization to ALBERT's parameter-efficient design (Liu et al., 2019). These models demonstrated remarkable capabilities in tasks ranging from question answering to text classification, while also revealing insights into how neural networks process and represent language.

Transfer learning emerged as a crucial technique in the deployment of these large models, fundamentally changing how AI systems are developed and deployed. This approach allowed models pre-trained on vast datasets to be fine-tuned for specific tasks with relatively little additional data, dramatically reducing the computational and data requirements for new applications. The emergence of few-shot and zero-shot learning capabilities further demonstrated these models' ability to adapt to new tasks with minimal or no explicit instruction, suggesting a form of meta-learning that more closely resembles human cognitive flexibility (Brown et al., 2020).

The field subsequently expanded beyond text to embrace multimodal models capable of processing and generating across different forms of media. This evolution was marked by the development of architectures that could seamlessly integrate different types of data, from images and audio to video and structured information. DALL-E demonstrated the possibility of generating images from textual descriptions, while models like GPT-4V showed capabilities in understanding and reasoning about visual information alongside text. Stable Diffusion introduced new techniques for efficient image generation, making these capabilities more accessible to researchers and developers (Ramesh et al., 2022).

The impact of this multimodal expansion has been profound, enabling new applications in creative tools, scientific visualization, and human-computer interaction. These models demonstrate an ability to understand and generate across modalities in ways that more closely approximate human cognitive capabilities. The development of controllable generation techniques has also enabled more precise and reliable outputs, addressing earlier challenges in consistency and coherence.

Recent architectural innovations have focused on improving efficiency and controllability while maintaining performance. The development of sparse attention mechanisms, such as those used in Longformer and

BigBird, has enabled processing of much longer sequences while reducing computational requirements. Meanwhile, techniques for controlling and steering generation have become more sophisticated, enabling more reliable and purposeful outputs (Zaheer et al., 2020).

These advances represent significant steps toward more general artificial intelligence, though important challenges remain. Issues of bias, reliability, and computational efficiency continue to drive research into more sophisticated architectures and training methods. The field has also begun to grapple with questions of model interpretability and control, as these systems become increasingly capable and widely deployed.

PRESENT CHALLENGES AND FUTURE CONCERNS

Despite remarkable advances in artificial intelligence, the field faces significant challenges that threaten its sustainable development and equitable deployment. These challenges span environmental, economic, technical, and societal dimensions, requiring careful consideration and systematic solutions.

The environmental impact of training large AI models has emerged as a pressing concern within the scientific community. Contemporary research reveals the substantial carbon footprint associated with developing and deploying advanced AI systems. A single training run for a large language model can produce carbon emissions equivalent to hundreds of cars' yearly output, with some estimates suggesting emissions of up to 626,000 pounds of carbon dioxide equivalent (Strubell et al., 2019). This environmental cost stems from the massive computational resources required for model training, which often involves multiple experimental iterations and increasingly larger architectures.

The hardware infrastructure supporting AI development presents another critical challenge. The global semiconductor shortage has exposed vulnerabilities in the supply chain for AI-specific computing hardware. This scarcity affects everything from graphics processing units (GPUs) to specialized AI accelerators, leading to increased costs and delayed research timelines. Manufacturing constraints, particularly in advanced semiconductor nodes, have created bottlenecks in the production of AI-optimized chips. Furthermore, geopolitical tensions surrounding semiconductor manufacturing and export controls threaten to fragment the global AI research community and impede collaborative development (Khan, 2022).

Data scarcity and quality present increasingly significant obstacles as the field advances. While early AI development benefited from readily available datasets, the quest for high-quality training data has become increasingly competitive. Previously accessible data sources are becoming exhausted, particularly in specialized domains and languages with limited digital presence. This scarcity disproportionately affects research in low-resource languages and specialized scientific fields, where annotated datasets are particularly scarce. The problem extends beyond mere quantity to questions of data quality, representativeness, and ethical considerations in data collection (Sambasivan et al., 2021).

The economic dimension of AI development has created concerning patterns of concentration. The computational and financial resources required for training and deploying state-of-the-art AI models have skyrocketed, with estimates suggesting that training a single large language model can cost millions of dollars. This economic barrier has led to a concentration of AI capabilities in the hands of a few well-resourced organizations, primarily large technology companies and elite research institutions. This concentration raises concerns about access equity and the diversity of perspectives in AI development (Ahmed & Wahed, 2020).

Technical challenges persist in scaling AI systems effectively. While larger models have demonstrated impressive capabilities, they also exhibit limitations in reasoning, reliability, and robustness. The phenomenon of model brittleness—where seemingly capable systems fail unexpectedly on edge cases—remains a significant concern. Additionally, current architectures struggle with problems requiring common-sense reasoning or causal understanding, despite their strong performance on pattern recognition tasks (Pearl & Mackenzie, 2018).

Infrastructure limitations pose another significant challenge. The increasing size of AI models strains existing computing infrastructure, network bandwidth, and storage systems. The demands of distributed training across data centers require sophisticated orchestration systems and high-bandwidth networking, while model deployment faces challenges in latency and resource efficiency. These infrastructure requirements further exacerbate the concentration of AI capabilities among well-resourced organizations.

Privacy and security concerns have also emerged as critical challenges. The need for large-scale data collection and sharing must be balanced against individual privacy rights and data protection regulations. Additionally, the potential for AI systems to be compromised or misused raises significant security concerns, particularly as these systems are deployed in sensitive applications (Papernot et al., 2018).

The challenge of reproducibility in AI research has become increasingly apparent. The combination of large-scale computational requirements, proprietary datasets, and complex training procedures makes it difficult for researchers to verify and build upon published results. This reproducibility crisis threatens the field's scientific foundations and impedes progress in addressing other technical challenges (Pineau et al., 2021).

The Road Ahead: Balancing Innovation and Responsibility

The future of AI development must navigate between continued innovation and responsible stewardship of resources. Research into more efficient training methods, such as sparse attention mechanisms and smaller, more specialized models, offers promise for reducing computational demands. Hardware innovations in neuromorphic computing and quantum processors may provide new paths to energy-efficient AI systems.

Democratizing AI access requires addressing both technical and economic barriers. Open-source initiatives, federated learning approaches, and improved model compression techniques can help distribute AI capabilities more widely. International collaboration frameworks for sharing research, data, and computational resources could help prevent a dangerous concentration of AI capabilities.

The field must also embrace responsible innovation practices. This includes developing robust safety measures, ensuring AI systems respect privacy and human rights, and creating governance frameworks that promote beneficial AI development while managing risks. The lessons of the AI Winter remind us that sustainable progress requires balancing ambition with pragmatism, ensuring that AI development serves humanity's broader interests rather than narrow technical achievements.

As we move forward, the key challenge will be maintaining the current momentum while addressing these fundamental challenges. Success will require unprecedented cooperation between researchers, industry leaders, policymakers, and the broader public to ensure that AI's potential is realized in a way that benefits all of humanity.

CONCLUSION

The history of artificial intelligence reflects a recurring cycle of high ambitions followed by periods of disillusionment. The AI Winter taught critical lessons about managing expectations, emphasizing the importance of pragmatic goals and incremental progress. AI's recent renaissance has emerged from the convergence of increased computational power, vast data resources, and significant algorithmic breakthroughs. Today, as generative AI propels the field toward new frontiers, the lessons from past winters remain relevant—highlighting the necessity of balancing innovation with realistic expectations, addressing challenges such as environmental sustainability, equitable access, and maintaining rigorous standards. Going forward, continued collaboration across disciplines, alongside responsible stewardship, will be essential to ensure AI's transformative potential benefits society broadly and sustainably.

REFERENCES

Ahmed, N., & Wahed, M. (2020). *The de-democratization of AI: Deep learning and the compute divide in artificial intelligence research.* arXiv preprint arXiv:2010.15581.

Boden, M. A. (2016). *AI: Its nature and future.* Oxford University Press.

Brooks, R. A. (1991). Intelligence without representation. *Artificial Intelligence, 47*(1–3), 139–159.

Brown, T. B., Mann, B., Ryder, N., Subbiah, M., Kaplan, J., Dhariwal, P., et al. (2020). Language models are few-shot learners. *Advances in Neural Information Processing Systems, 33*, 1877–1901.

Crevier, D. (1993). *AI: The tumultuous history of the search for artificial intelligence.* Basic Books.

Deng, J., Dong, W., Socher, R., Li, L. J., Li, K., & Fei-Fei, L. (2009). ImageNet: A large-scale hierarchical image database. In *IEEE conference on computer vision and pattern recognition* (pp. 248–255).

Dennett, D. C. (2017). *From bacteria to bach and back: The evolution of minds.* W.W. Norton & Company.

Devlin, J., Chang, M. W., Lee, K., & Toutanova, K. (2019). BERT: Pre-training of deep bidirectional transformers for language understanding. *Proceedings of NAACL-HLT, 2019,* 4171–4186.

Dong, X. L., & Srivastava, D. (2013). Big data integration. In *IEEE international conference on data engineering* (pp. 1245–1248).

Dreyfus, H. L. (1972). *What computers can't do: A critique of artificial reason.* Harper & Row.

Floridi, L. (2019). *The ethics of artificial intelligence.* Oxford University Press.

Goodfellow, I., Pouget-Abadie, J., Mirza, M., Xu, B., Warde-Farley, D., Ozair, S., et al. (2014). Generative adversarial nets. *Advances in Neural Information Processing Systems,* 2672–2680.

Goodfellow, I., Bengio, Y., & Courville, A. (2016). *Deep learning.* MIT Press.

He, K., Zhang, X., Ren, S., & Sun, J. (2016). Deep residual learning for image recognition. In *IEEE conference on computer vision and pattern recognition* (pp. 770–778).

Hendler, J. (2008). Avoiding another AI winter. *IEEE Intelligent Systems, 23*(2), 2–4.

Hillis, W. D. (1985). *The connection machine.* MIT Press.

Hochreiter, S., & Schmidhuber, J. (1997). Long short-term memory. *Neural Computation, 9*(8), 1735–1780.

Jonas, E., Schleier-Smith, J., Sreekanti, V., et al. (2019). *Cloud programming simplified: A Berkeley view on serverless computing.* arXiv preprint arXiv:1902.03383.

Jouppi, N. P., Young, C., Patil, N., et al. (2017). In-datacenter performance analysis of a tensor processing unit. In *ACM/IEEE international symposium on computer architecture* (pp. 1–12).

Kaplan, J., McCandlish, S., Henighan, T., Brown, T. B., Chess, B., Child, R., et al. (2020). *Scaling laws for neural language models.* arXiv preprint arXiv:2001.08361.

Khan, S. (2022). The semiconductor crisis: Implications for AI development and global tech policy. *Journal of Technology Policy, 15*(2), 78–96.

Kirk, D. B., & Hwu, W. M. W. (2017). *Programming massively parallel processors: A hands-on approach.* Morgan Kaufmann.

Krizhevsky, A., Sutskever, I., & Hinton, G. E. (2012). ImageNet classification with deep convolutional neural networks. *Advances in Neural Information Processing Systems,* 1097–1105.

LeCun, Y., Bengio, Y., & Hinton, G. (2015). Deep learning. *Nature, 521*(7553), 436–444.

Lighthill, J. (1973). *Artificial intelligence: A general survey.* Science Research Council.

Liu, Y., Ott, M., Goyal, N., Du, J., Joshi, M., Chen, D., et al. (2019). *RoBERTa: A robustly optimized BERT pretraining approach.* arXiv preprint arXiv:1907.11692.

McCarthy, J., Minsky, M. L., Rochester, N., & Shannon, C. E. (1955). A proposal for the Dartmouth summer research project on artificial intelligence. *AI Magazine, 27*(4), 12–14.

McCorduck, P. (2004). *Machines who think: A personal inquiry into the history and prospects of artificial intelligence* (2nd ed.). A K Peters.

McDermott, J. (1982). R1: A rule-based configurer of computer systems. *Artificial Intelligence, 19*(1), 39–88.

Newell, A., & Simon, H. A. (1956). The logic theory machine: A complex information processing system. RAND Corporation, P-868.

Newell, A., Shaw, J. C., & Simon, H. A. (1959). Report on a general problem-solving program. In *Proceedings of the international conference on information processing* (pp. 256–264).

Nilsson, N. J. (2009). *The quest for artificial intelligence: A history of ideas and achievements*. Cambridge University Press.

NVIDIA. (2018). *NVIDIA turing GPU architecture whitepaper*. Technical report.

Oh, K. S., & Jung, K. (2004). GPU implementation of neural networks. *Pattern Recognition, 37*(6), 1311–1314.

Papernot, N., McDaniel, P., Sinha, A., & Wellman, M. (2018). Towards the science of security and privacy in machine learning. *IEEE Security and Privacy, 16*(4), 67–82.

Pearl, J., & Mackenzie, D. (2018). *The book of why: The new science of cause and effect*. Basic Books.

Pineau, J., Vincent-Lamarre, P., Sinha, K., Larivière, V., Beygelzimer, A., d'Alché-Buc, F., et al. (2021). Improving reproducibility in machine learning research. *Journal of Machine Learning Research, 22*(93), 1–5.

Ramesh, A., Dhariwal, P., Nichol, A., Chu, C., & Chen, M. (2022). *Hierarchical text-conditional image generation with CLIP latents*. arXiv preprint arXiv:2204.06125.

Roland, A., & Shiman, P. (2002). *Strategic computing: DARPA and the quest for machine intelligence, 1983–1993*. MIT Press.

Russell, S., & Norvig, P. (2020). *Artificial intelligence: A modern approach* (4th ed.). Pearson.

Sambasivan, N., Kapania, S., Highfill, H., Akrong, D., Paritosh, P., & Aroyo, L. M. (2021). "Everyone wants to do the model work, not the data work": Data cascades in high-stakes AI. In *Proceedings of the 2021 CHI conference on human factors in computing systems* (pp. 1–15).

Sejnowski, T. J. (2018). *The deep learning revolution*. MIT Press.

Strubell, E., Ganesh, A., & McCallum, A. (2019). Energy and policy considerations for deep learning in NLP. In *Proceedings of the 57th annual meeting of the association for computational linguistics* (pp. 3645–3650).

Turing, A. M. (1950). Computing machinery and intelligence. *Mind, 59*(236), 433–460.

Vaswani, A., Shazeer, N., Parmar, N., Uszkoreit, J., Jones, L., Gomez, A. N., et al. (2017). Attention is all you need. In *Advances in neural information processing systems* (pp. 5998–6008).

Weizenbaum, J. (1966). ELIZA—A computer program for the study of natural language communication between man and machine. *Communications of the ACM, 9*(1), 36–45.

Winograd, T. (1972). Understanding natural language. *Cognitive Psychology, 3*(1), 1–191.

Zaheer, M., Guruganesh, G., Dubey, K. A., Ainslie, J., Alberti, C., Ontanon, S., et al. (2020). Big bird: Transformers for longer sequences. *Advances in Neural Information Processing Systems, 33*, 17283–17297.

CHAPTER 3

Generative AI for Research

Abstract This chapter explores how generative AI is reshaping the academic research lifecycle—from ideation and literature discovery to hypothesis formation, methodological planning, and data acquisition. By enhancing early-stage processes through tools like GPT, Claude, and Gemini, researchers can streamline conceptual development, uncover cross-disciplinary connections, and rapidly synthesize literature. Generative AI assists in hypothesis generation and method selection, offers technical support for coding and data collection, and facilitates integration across tools. However, its value lies not in automation alone but in collaboration: when used critically, these systems enhance scholarly insight without compromising academic rigor. The chapter emphasizes the importance of validation, transparency, and ethical caution in AI-assisted research design.

Keywords Generative AI • Academic research • Literature review • Hypothesis generation • Research methodology

The academic research lifecycle traditionally proceeds through a series of interconnected phases—initial ideation, literature review, hypothesis generation, data collection, analysis, writing, and dissemination (Creswell, 2014). Each step demands substantial cognitive effort, creative thinking, methodological precision, and analytical rigor from researchers. The

E. Haber et al., *Using AI in Academic Writing and Research*, https://doi.org/10.1007/978-3-031-91705-9_3

emergence of generative AI, particularly advanced large language models (LLMs) such as GPT (OpenAI), Claude (Anthropic), Llama (Meta), or Gemini (Google), is fundamentally transforming how scholars approach these early stages of inquiry, offering innovative pathways for ideation, conceptual framing, and methodological exploration.

The traditional research process, while methodologically sound, faces significant limitations in today's rapidly evolving academic world. Researchers must navigate an increasingly complex web of interdisciplinary connections, manage exponentially growing bodies of literature, and identify novel contributions in increasingly specialized fields. In adjacent fields, such as professional writing, researchers utilizing generative AI tools report up to a 40 percent reduction in task time and significant quality improvements (Noy & Zhang, 2023). These efficiency gains offer a compelling analogue for the potential benefits of GenAI in early-stage academic research, and are particularly pronounced in interdisciplinary research, where AI tools excel at identifying cross-domain connections that might otherwise remain unexplored.

Recent scholarly discourse emphasizes that generative AI serves not as a replacement for researcher expertise, but as an augmentative force that enhances human intellectual capabilities (van Dis et al., 2023; Rossi et al., 2024). This synergistic relationship has been documented across various disciplines, from social sciences to medical research, where AI-assisted research design has led to more comprehensive and nuanced research questions (Borger et al., 2023; Oksanen, 2024). For instance, researchers can leverage generative AI tools to generate multiple perspectives on research problems, rapidly synthesize existing literature, and identify potential methodological approaches—all while maintaining critical human oversight of the process.

The integration of generative AI aligns with the reality of today's data-rich, dynamic, and increasingly global academic environment (Chen et al., 2021). The volume of published research has grown exponentially, with some fields doubling their literature base every few years (Bornmann & Mutz, 2015; Bornmann et al., 2021). This information explosion makes traditional manual approaches to literature review and concept development both time-consuming and prone to oversight. AI-driven approaches have demonstrated particular value in identifying emerging research trends and gaps, with studies showing that AI-assisted literature reviews can identify more relevant sources than traditional methods alone and lead to significant time savings when used correctly (van Dijk et al., 2023). However, maintaining a balanced and critical perspective remains crucial. While these tools can recommend new angles or reveal potential theoretical frameworks, they should be employed as aids rather than arbiters of research direction. One of the key challenges includes less critical thinking and authenticity (Cardon et al., 2023): after all, generative AI is, well, generative and, by design, geared toward the repetition of patterns.

Scholars must also remain attuned to issues of bias, transparency, and intellectual integrity (Thorp, 2023). Generative AI reflects the existing social biases and frequently amplifies them to larger orders of magnitude (Gorska & Jemielniak, 2023). The integration of generative AI into the research lifecycle represents a significant opportunity for enhancing scholarly work, provided it is implemented thoughtfully and ethically. Practical applications include using AI to generate initial research questions, identify relevant theoretical frameworks, or suggest methodological approaches. Researchers are encouraged to maintain detailed documentation of AI interactions, critically evaluate AI-generated suggestions, and regularly validate findings against established academic standards.

IDEATION AND CONCEPTUAL DEVELOPMENT

At the earliest stage of a research project, scholars often need to be herding cats: navigate a complex landscape of broad interests, partial knowledge, and emergent themes. The traditional process of transforming disparate ideas into coherent research problems has historically relied on researchers' creativity, disciplinary expertise, and methodical exploration of existing literature (Creswell, 2014; Amabile, 1983). Generative AI now offers sophisticated pathways to enhance and streamline these initial conceptual processes, serving as an advanced ideation tool that illuminates novel connections, identifies unexplored territories, and helps crystallize preliminary concepts into focused research questions.

Large language models (LLMs) can synthesize information from extensive textual databases, revealing potential research directions that might remain hidden during conventional literature reviews (Floridi & Chiriatti, 2020; van Dis et al., 2023). These systems facilitate what we might term "augmented ideation," complementing rather than supplanting researchers' intellectual contributions. Contemporary experiments demonstrate that generative AI functions as a catalyst for creative thinking, offering alternative theoretical frameworks, revealing cross-disciplinary connections, and challenging researchers' assumptions through counterfactual analysis (Rudolph et al., 2023; Boden, 2009).

Consider a researcher investigating the societal implications of AI in education. They might uncover diverse analytical perspectives through generative AI—from comparative policy studies across jurisdictions to investigations of teacher training paradigms in AI adoption or historical analyses of technological integration in educational settings. The AI system can efficiently process vast datasets to identify emerging patterns, pose methodological questions, and highlight recent empirical findings that could enrich the researcher's conceptual framework. This acceleration of the exploratory phase enables a swifter progression toward hypothesis formulation. However, judicious application remains paramount. While generative AI excels at proposing novel research directions, it may also generate tangential, theoretically unsound, or ethically problematic suggestions if accepted without critical evaluation (Thorp, 2023; Lenharo, 2024). Researchers must maintain rigorous analytical standards, treating AI-generated outputs as preliminary insights requiring thorough examination, validation, and refinement. The objective is to enhance, not outsource, the intellectual process, ensuring that human expertise, domain knowledge, and academic judgment guide research conceptualization. Generative AI emerges as an invaluable collaborative tool in shaping contemporary research landscapes. By revealing unexplored possibilities, questioning established assumptions, and fostering interdisciplinary dialogue, these systems enhance the ideation and conceptual development phase's efficiency, creativity, and robustness. The following sections examine how these initial advantages complement literature review processes, hypothesis development, and methodological planning, establishing a foundation for comprehensive empirical investigation.

Literature Discovery and Rapid Reviews

Contemporary researchers face an unprecedented challenge in managing the aforementioned exponential growth of scholarly publications. This "information explosion" presents significant obstacles in identifying seminal works, understanding cutting-edge developments, and recognizing the intellectual patterns that define academic fields (Bornmann et al., 2021). Advanced generative AI models, leveraging sophisticated natural language processing capabilities, offer innovative solutions for navigating this complexity, enabling more systematic and efficient approaches to literature discovery and review.

These AI-powered tools excel at preliminary content filtration, efficiently identifying crucial publications and datasets that align with a project's theoretical framework (Floridi & Chiriatti, 2020). Researchers can leverage generative models through targeted prompting to identify foundational studies, recognize influential scholars, and map conceptual clusters. This approach dramatically reduces the time traditionally required for comprehensive literature reviews while potentially uncovering valuable connections that might escape manual analysis (van Dis et al., 2023). The effectiveness of computational approaches in systematic reviews has been well-documented across diverse disciplines, from public health to social sciences (Tsafnat et al., 2014; Baker & Dunbar, 2020).

A distinctive strength of generative models is their ability to synthesize extensive scholarly work while preserving essential nuances and contextual relationships. Following the previous example of a researcher exploring the intersection of AI ethics and higher education, through carefully crafted prompts, they can rapidly generate comprehensive overviews of key debates—from privacy concerns to algorithmic bias in admissions—while identifying areas lacking empirical support or theoretical development. This dynamic approach represents a significant advancement over traditional linear review methods, which often require extensive periods of reading and synthesis.

However, integrating AI into literature reviews demands careful consideration and methodological rigor. Generative models may occasionally produce inaccurate information or misattribute sources, necessitating thorough verification of AI-generated content. Every single reference suggested by an AI model has to be checked and reviewed: not only sometimes they do not cover exactly what the model suggested they would, but they may even not exist at all, despite plausibly looking DOIs, page number ranges, or links. Thus, maintaining scholarly integrity requires systematic validation of sources, careful verification of citations, and critical evaluation of AI-generated syntheses.

Generative AI fundamentally enhances researchers' capabilities to rapidly develop a comprehensive understanding of new or evolving fields. By streamlining the identification and synthesis of relevant scholarship, these tools enable a more strategic allocation of research resources. When implemented thoughtfully, AI assistance can transform literature review from a time-intensive necessity into an agile, iterative process that generates more profound insights and facilitates more innovative research directions. It is unlikely, though, that any time soon, literature reviews will be run automatically and unsupervised.

Hypothesis Generation and Preliminary Frameworks

The transition from broad thematic exploration to precisely testable hypotheses represents a critical juncture in the research process. Traditionally, scholars have relied on theoretical foundations, disciplinary expertise, and methodical iteration to develop hypotheses (Bryman, 2012; Maxwell, 2013). Generative AI now offers powerful complementary capabilities that enhance this process without supplanting the researcher's essential role. These advanced systems excel at suggesting logical extensions of established theories, identifying subtle variable relationships, and illuminating potential causal mechanisms that might otherwise remain unexplored, catalyzing more sophisticated research design.

Consider a researcher investigating the impact of digital literacy programs on community development. After analyzing relevant theoretical constructs and empirical findings, a generative AI system might propose nuanced hypotheses that account for contextual factors:

> In regions with lower baseline educational attainment, digital literacy training will demonstrate a stronger positive effect on entrepreneurial activity compared to regions with abundant educational resources.

This suggestion compels researchers to examine how socioeconomic contexts moderate program outcomes, potentially revealing complex interaction effects that merit investigation. Similarly, in organizational research, AI might highlight specific mediating mechanisms:

> In remote work environments, the presence of structured communication channels mediates the relationship between transformational leadership styles and team cohesion.

Drawing attention to variables that researchers might have initially overlooked, these capabilities align with evolving research practices that increasingly integrate predictive analytics and data-driven methods in hypothesis formation (Shmueli, 2010). By analyzing extensive corpora of academic literature, large language models can surface plausible connections, highlight underutilized theoretical constructs, and suggest novel analytical frameworks. For instance, in public health research, a generative model might propose examining how "community trust in healthcare providers" or "cultural alignment of health messaging" mediates intervention effectiveness, inspiring more sophisticated conceptual frameworks. Researchers can then systematically evaluate these factors through established qualitative and quantitative methods, moving beyond initial theoretical speculation (Robson & McCartan, 2016; Ciesielska & Jemielniak, 2018). However, rigorous scholarly judgment remains paramount in this process. Not every AI-generated hypothesis will withstand theoretical scrutiny or align with existing empirical evidence (Maxwell, 2013). Some suggestions may venture into speculative territory or reflect inherent biases in the underlying training data. Consequently, hypotheses derived through AI assistance must undergo careful evaluation against established theoretical frameworks, methodological constraints, and available empirical evidence.

The researcher's expertise—informed by deep domain knowledge and scholarly rigor—remains the ultimate arbiter of a hypothesis' validity and potential significance. The strategic integration of generative AI in hypothesis development can significantly enhance research design by accelerating the identification of testable relationships, revealing unexpected theoretical connections, and encouraging more sophisticated conceptual frameworks. When properly implemented, AI-assisted hypothesis generation enriches the research process, helping scholars move from initial concepts to well-structured, testable propositions. This approach combines the breadth of AI-driven analysis with the depth of human expertise, ultimately strengthening the foundation for subsequent empirical investigation. The result is a more robust and nuanced research design that benefits from both technological capabilities and scholarly judgment, setting the stage for meaningful scientific contributions.

EARLY METHODOLOGICAL GUIDANCE

The selection of appropriate research methods, following the establishment of research direction and preliminary hypotheses, represents a crucial decision point in the research process. While methodological selection has traditionally been guided by disciplinary conventions, theoretical foundations, and researchers' methodological expertise (Flick, 2018; Gerring, 2017), generative AI now offers sophisticated guidance to navigate the complex landscape of qualitative, quantitative, and mixed-methods approaches, potentially enhancing the methodological decision-making process. Especially in mixed methods, such as the *Thick Big Data* method (Jemielniak, 2020), using AI to fill the gaps in methodologies we are not experts in can be really beneficial and provide a more rounded approach to the studied phenomenon. AI tools can also propose exploratory data science pilot studies, which can be easily deployed—again, by using AI coding agent support.

Consider a researcher investigating public trust in science who faces the choice between in-depth interviews, large-scale surveys, or an integrated approach. Through interaction with a generative AI system, the researcher can articulate their study's key requirements—such as the need for both contextual understanding and statistical generalizability. The AI might suggest a sophisticated mixed-methods design incorporating initial qualitative interviews to explore trust narratives across different communities, followed by a quantitative survey to assess the prevalence of identified patterns. This guidance aligns with established methodological literature advocating for the complementarity of multiple methods in addressing complex research questions (Johnson & Onwuegbuzie, 2004; Tashakkori et al., 2021).

As mentioned, generative AI is valuable in introducing researchers to specialized methodological approaches that may lie outside their immediate expertise. For instance, a researcher examining environmental policy discourse might benefit from AI suggestions combining traditional qualitative content analysis with advanced computational techniques such as topic modeling or sentiment analysis. Such recommendations can encourage methodological innovation while maintaining analytical rigor, bridging interpretive depth with data-driven insights (Flick, 2018).

For qualitative studies, AI can illuminate emerging methodological innovations beyond conventional approaches. Researchers might discover the applicability of participatory action research, visual ethnography, or digital anthropology to their specific research contexts. In quantitative domains, AI can identify sophisticated statistical techniques or experimental designs that precisely align with research objectives—perhaps suggesting longitudinal mixed-effects models for educational intervention studies or advocating for robust non-parametric approaches when data violate traditional assumptions.

However, methodological selection must remain grounded in practical considerations. While generative AI excels at identifying potential methodological approaches, researchers must carefully evaluate suggestions against real-world constraints, including available expertise, resources, temporal limitations, and ethical considerations. The AI's recommendations, derived from patterns in existing literature and training data, require careful validation against specific research contexts. Scholars must exercise professional judgment to ensure that selected methods align with research objectives and remain feasible and ethically sound within their particular research environment.

Generative AI thus serves as a sophisticated methodological consultant during research planning, illuminating innovative approaches while encouraging critical reflection on methodological choices. Through strategic engagement with AI-generated suggestions, researchers can develop robust, contextually appropriate, and innovative methodological frameworks that effectively guide subsequent phases of data collection, analysis, and interpretation. This synthesis of technological capability and scholarly judgment enhances the potential for methodological innovation while maintaining essential standards of academic rigor.

Automated Tool Development and Data Acquisition

The transition from research design to data collection represents a critical juncture where technical implementation meets methodological planning. While researchers have traditionally invested significant time in developing custom research instruments, programming data collection tools, and managing complex data integration processes (Munzert et al., 2015), generative AI now offers sophisticated assistance in streamlining these technical aspects of research preparation. These advanced systems can generate customized code, suggest efficient data collection strategies, and facilitate the development of integrated research workflows.

Consider a researcher investigating public policy evolution through governmental documentation. Rather than manually crafting web scraping scripts, they might leverage code-generating AI systems to develop efficient data collection protocols. By providing specific parameters—such as target repositories, document specifications, and extraction criteria—researchers can obtain sophisticated Python scripts that handle web requests, manage pagination, and structure data output (Chen et al., 2021). This automation accelerates development and allows researchers to focus on crucial aspects like ethical compliance, data quality assurance, and methodological refinement.

The capabilities of generative AI extend beyond basic data collection to sophisticated preprocessing and analysis preparation. For instance, when preparing textual data for computational analysis, researchers can obtain AI-generated code snippets for advanced natural language processing tasks—including tokenization, syntactic parsing, or sentiment analysis. Similarly, when interfacing with social media APIs, these systems can provide robust templates for authentication, rate limiting, and data parsing. This technical assistance enables researchers to bridge the gap between conceptual requirements and practical implementation more efficiently.

The AI's capacity to facilitate integration across diverse technical environments is particularly valuable. Modern research often demands fluency in multiple programming languages and analytical frameworks. Generative AI can suggest efficient solutions for data transfer between different platforms—for example, connecting R-based statistical analyses with Python-based data collection systems. This integration support reduces technical barriers and accelerates the development of comprehensive research workflows.

Given that more and more tools rely on low-code or no-code approaches, using AI for data acquisition and research will likely become a standard of the academic repertoire (Ciechanowski et al., 2020).

CONCLUSION

Generative AI has profoundly reshaped the academic research process, streamlining ideation, literature reviews, hypothesis formation, methodological selection, and data acquisition. By providing tools for efficient exploration, hypothesis refinement, methodological consultation, and technical automation, generative AI significantly reduces the time and cognitive burden traditionally associated with research design and data collection. Nevertheless, successful integration requires critical human oversight, as AI-generated insights must always be validated against theoretical rigor, empirical evidence, and ethical considerations. Ultimately, generative AI emerges not as a substitute but as a valuable partner—augmenting researchers' capabilities and enabling them to focus more deeply on the creative and intellectual aspects of scholarship.

REFERENCES

Amabile, T. M. (1983). The social psychology of creativity: A componential conceptualization. *Journal of Personality and Social Psychology, 45*(2), 357–376.
Baker, S., & Dunbar, M. (2020). Using text mining for identifying research gaps in systematic reviews. *Journal of Information Science, 46*(1), 3–16.
Boden, M. A. (2009). Computer models of creativity. *AI Magazine, 30*(3), 23–34.

Borger, J. G., Ng, A. P., Anderton, H., Ashdown, G. W., Auld, M., Blewitt, M. E., Brown, D. V., et al. (2023). Artificial intelligence takes center stage: Exploring the capabilities and implications of ChatGPT and other AI-assisted technologies in scientific research and education. *Immunology and Cell Biology, 101*(10), 923–935.

Bornmann, L., Haunschild, R., & Mutz, R. (2021). Growth rates of modern science: A latent piecewise growth curve approach to model publication numbers from established and new literature databases. *Humanities & Social Sciences Communications, 8*(1), 1–15.

Bornmann, L., & Mutz, R. (2015). Growth rates of modern science: A bibliometric analysis based on the number of publications and cited references: Growth rates of modern science: A bibliometric analysis based on the number of publications and cited references. *Journal of the Association for Information Science and Technology, 66*(11), 2215–2222.

Bryman, A. (2012). *Social research methods* (4th ed.). Oxford University Press.

Cardon, P., Fleischmann, C., Aritz, J., Logemann, M., & Heidewald, J. (2023). The challenges and opportunities of AI-assisted writing: Developing AI literacy for the AI age. *Business and Professional Communication Quarterly, 86*(3), 257–295.

Chen, M., Tworek, J., Jun, H., Yuan, Q., de Oliveira Pinto, H. P., Kaplan, J., Edwards, H., et al. 2021. *Evaluating large language models trained on code.* arXiv [cs.LG]. arXiv. http://arxiv.org/abs/2107.03374

Chen, T., Xu, B., Zhang, C., & Guestrin, C. (2021). A survey on large-scale deep learning: From neurons to neural architecture search. *IEEE Transactions on Pattern Analysis and Machine Intelligence, 43*(11), 3719–3737.

Ciechanowski, L., Jemielniak, D., & Gloor, P. A. (2020). AI research without coding: The art of fighting without fighting: Data science for qualitative researchers. *Journal of Business Research, 117*(September), 322–330.

Ciesielska, M., & Jemielniak, D. (Eds.). (2018). *Qualitative methodologies in organization studies: Theories and new approaches.* Palgrave Macmillan.

Creswell, J. W. (2014). *Research design: Qualitative, quantitative, and mixed methods approaches.* SAGE Publications.

Flick, U. (2018). *An introduction to qualitative research.* SAGE.

Floridi, L., & Chiriatti, M. (2020). GPT-3: Its nature, scope, limits, and consequences. *Minds and Machines, 30*(4), 681–694.

Gerring, J. (2017). *Strategies for social inquiry: Case study research: Principles and practices* (2nd ed.). Cambridge University Press.

Gorska, A. M., & Jemielniak, D. (2023). The invisible women: Uncovering gender bias in AI-generated images of professionals. *Feminist Media Studies, 23*(8), 4370–4375.

Jemielniak, D. (2020). *Thick Big Data: Doing digital social sciences.* Oxford University Press.

Johnson, R. B., & Onwuegbuzie, A. J. (2004). Mixed methods research: A research paradigm whose time has come. *Educational Researcher (Washington, D.C.: 1972), 33*(7), 14–26.

Lenharo, M. (2024). ChatGPT turns two: How the AI Chatbot has changed scientists' lives. *Nature, 636*(8042), 281–282.

Maxwell, J. A. (2013). *Qualitative research design: An interactive approach.* SAGE Publications.

Munzert, S., Rubba, C., Meißner, P., & Nyhuis, D. (2015). *Automated data collection with R: A practical guide to web scraping and text mining.* Wiley.

Noy, S., & Zhang, W. (2023). Experimental evidence on the productivity effects of generative artificial intelligence. *Science (New York, N.Y.), 381*(6654), 187–192.

Oksanen, J. (2024). Bridging the integrity gap: Towards AI-assisted design research. In *Extended abstracts of the CHI conference on human factors in computing systems* (pp. 1–5). ACM.

Robson, C., & McCartan, K. (2016). *Real world research. EPUB* (4th ed.). John Wiley & Sons. https://www.wiley.com/en-gb/Real+World+Research%2C+4th+Edition-p-9781119144854

Rossi, S., Rossi, M., Mukkamala, R. R., Thatcher, J. B., & Dwivedi, Y. K. (2024). Augmenting research methods with foundation models and generative AI. *International Journal of Information Management, 77*(102749), 102749.

Rudolph, J., Tan, S., & Tan, S. H. (2023). ChatGPT: Bullshit spewer or ultimate research assistant? *Journal of Surgical Research, 282*, 346–347.

Shmueli, G. (2010). To explain or to predict? *Statistical Science: A Review Journal of the Institute of Mathematical Statistics, 25*(3), 289–310.

Tashakkori, A., Teddlie, C., & SAGE Publications, Inc. (2021). *SAGE handbook of mixed methods in social & behavioral research* (2nd ed.). SAGE Publications.

Thorp, H. H. (2023). ChatGPT is fun, but not an author. *Science (New York, N.Y.), 379*(6630), 313.

Tsafnat, G., Glasziou, P., Choong, M. K., Dunn, A., Galgani, F., & Coiera, E. (2014). Systematic review automation technologies. *Systematic Reviews, 3*(1), 74.

van Dijk, S. H. B., Brusse-Keizer, M. G. J., Bucsán, C. C., van der Palen, J., Doggen, C. J. M., & Lenferink, A. (2023). Artificial intelligence in systematic reviews: Promising when appropriately used. *BMJ Open, 13*(7), e072254.

van Dis, E. A. M., Bollen, J., Zuidema, W., van Rooij, R., & Bockting, C. L. (2023). ChatGPT: Five priorities for research. *Nature, 614*(7947), 224–226.

CHAPTER 4

Writing and Publishing with Generative AI

Abstract This chapter examines how generative AI is transforming academic writing and publishing. It explores AI's role across the entire writing lifecycle—from overcoming writer's block and structuring arguments to refining prose, formatting citations, and preparing submissions. While AI accelerates drafting and revision through brainstorming, stylistic editing, and even simulated peer review, the chapter underscores that human oversight remains critical for intellectual depth, factual accuracy, and scholarly rigor. It also addresses the risks of over-reliance, including hallucinated citations and the erosion of academic voice, and offers practical strategies for integrating AI responsibly into writing workflows without compromising originality or integrity.

Keywords Academic writing • Generative AI • Scholarly publishing • Citation management • AI-assisted drafting

Writing with generative AI represents a transformative shift in academic practice. No longer must scholars stare at a blank screen, struggling to generate ideas or find the right way to begin an article or grant proposal. Generative AI tools can help overcome writer's block by providing structure, suggesting phrasing, and offering new angles for exploration. The impact extends far beyond mere text generation—it serves as a

E. Haber et al., *Using AI in Academic Writing and Research*, https://doi.org/10.1007/978-3-031-91705-9_4

multifaceted tool across the entire academic workflow. From brainstorming research questions and structuring arguments to drafting grant proposals, synthesizing literature reviews, and preparing research presentations, AI assists at every stage (Kulkarni et al., 2024). It can help craft conference abstracts, develop research methodologies, formulate hypotheses, refine theoretical frameworks, and identify potential research gaps within a field (Wagner et al., 2022). Additionally, these tools support academic project management by generating research timelines, creating curriculum materials, and formulating assessment rubrics. More than just a writing aid, generative AI is already reshaping the way academics think, plan, and execute their work, fundamentally altering the research and publication process (Dwivedi et al., 2023).

Despite its advancements, generative AI has not yet reached the point where a single prompt can produce a fully formed academic paper of publishable quality. Various attempts have been made to automate scholarly writing, including experimental efforts such as Stanford's STORM model, but anyone who has experimented with such systems quickly realizes their limitations (Kulkarni et al., 2024). While AI can generate coherent text and even insert citations, academic research and publishing require far more than assembling words in a structured format. A well-crafted paper is the product of rigorous analysis, critical engagement with the literature, methodological precision, and intellectual creativity—elements that AI, for now, cannot independently replicate (Milano et al., 2023). While the day may come when AI plays a larger role in research production, scholars still need to conduct the research, interpret findings, and construct arguments with depth and originality (Dwivedi et al., 2023).

This chapter explores the various ways generative AI can support academic writing while emphasizing the necessity of human oversight. We begin with the drafting process, examining how AI can assist in brainstorming, structuring, and refining text while ensuring that scholars maintain control over their intellectual contributions. Next, we turn to citations and references, discussing how AI can help format bibliographies, manage citation styles, and cross-check sources while also addressing potential risks such as hallucinated references (Milano et al., 2023). Finally, we explore strategies for optimizing publication, including how AI can help align manuscripts with journal guidelines, analyze recent publications to match editorial expectations, and assist in crafting submission materials such as abstracts and cover letters. Throughout, we underscore the importance of human judgment in ensuring that AI remains a tool for enhancement rather than a substitute for critical thinking and academic rigor.

THE DRAFTING PROCESS

Writing is often a challenging task, even for experienced academics. The well-known phenomenon of writer's block is not exclusive to creative writing; it frequently affects academic work as well. How many times have you stared at a blank screen, struggling to start, continue, or conclude a research paper, grant proposal, or any other academic text? The good news is that generative AI can help overcome these hurdles (Grimes et al., 2023). Whether you are drafting an article, conceptualizing a research grant, or structuring a dissertation, AI tools can assist at every stage of the writing process. No longer must you be paralyzed by the daunting prospect of a blank page or an incomplete argument—AI can provide structure, generate ideas, and refine your writing efficiently.

Of course, the way AI assists in drafting will vary depending on the type of academic writing. Composing a research paper differs from writing a grant proposal, and both could differ from drafting a book chapter or a conference abstract. However, the fundamental principles remain the same: AI can serve as a brainstorming partner, an initial text generator, and a refinement tool. While the specific techniques may vary, the key takeaway is that generative AI is not a replacement for the author's critical thinking and expertise but rather a tool that can streamline and enhance the writing process (Cotton et al., 2024).

It is important to first clarify that while AI is a powerful writing tool, relying on it to generate entire sections from scratch is not advisable. The temptation to simply input a prompt such as "Write me a full research proposal on X" and receive a well-structured, seemingly coherent response can be strong. In some cases, a sufficiently detailed prompt may yield text that follows the expected guidelines. However, while such output may be readable, it is unlikely to be truly useful. AI-generated drafts frequently lack depth, originality, and meaningful engagement with the subject matter (Holmes, 2023). Rather than streamlining the writing process, this approach can ultimately be counterproductive—requiring extensive revisions, restructuring, and refinement to meet scholarly standards. A more effective strategy is to treat AI as an assistant that enhances and refines original ideas, rather than as a ghostwriter replacing intellectual effort.

Instead of treating AI as a substitute for writing, a more effective approach is to begin with a brainstorming phase, as we discussed in an earlier chapter. Engaging with AI as a thought partner allows you to refine ideas, explore alternative perspectives, and develop a structured plan before drafting. Choose a tool that best suits your needs—whether it is ChatGPT, Claude, or another generative AI system—and provide as much relevant context as possible. Think of AI as a highly skilled research assistant or even a collaborative peer—one that, while prone to occasional errors (which we will address later), is always available for discussion, eager to refine your work, and capable of generating new insights that can help sharpen your research (Stokel-Walker, 2023). By actively engaging with AI rather than passively accepting its outputs, you can maximize its potential as a tool for enhancing academic writing.

Give the generative AI tool as much context as possible. The more information you provide, the more precise and relevant its output will be. Outline what you want to write about, articulate your thesis, and specify key arguments or themes. If you already have a partial draft, include it—either by attaching it or pasting it directly into the AI tool. Mention any relevant literature, theories, or frameworks you plan to engage with so that AI can tailor its suggestions accordingly (Barros et al., 2023). AI is most effective when it has substantial input to work with rather than being asked to generate content from scratch. By treating it as an extension of your own thought process rather than a shortcut, you can ensure that its contributions align more closely with your academic goals.

During this brainstorming process, however, it is important to recognize a common limitation of generative AI: it tends to agree with you too readily. If you present an idea, the AI will often respond with **"That's a terrific idea!"** or generate supportive reasoning without critically engaging with your argument. This can create a false sense of validation, making it seem as though your approach is unassailable. However, genuine academic writing thrives on intellectual rigor and challenge. To counterbalance this tendency, you must actively push back against the AI's affirmations. Explicitly instruct it to critique your ideas, identify counterarguments, or highlight potential weaknesses in your reasoning. For instance, you can prompt: **"Challenge my thesis by identifying gaps in my argument or existing literature that contradicts my claim."** This practice helps ensure that the AI is not just reinforcing your perspective but actively assisting in refining and strengthening your work.

Once you have explored your ideas through brainstorming, the next step is to structure your writing. Before diving into full paragraphs, consider the overall framework of your paper, proposal, or chapter. How long do you expect it to be? Are you writing for a specific journal, funding body, or academic audience? What are the main sections and sub-sections? AI tools can be particularly helpful in this phase. You can ask them to suggest an outline based on the information you've provided: **"Given my thesis and main arguments, propose a structured outline for a journal article"** or **"Based on my research topic, suggest a logical chapter breakdown."** While AI-generated outlines should never be followed blindly, they can serve as a useful starting point, prompting you to consider organizational structures you may not have thought of otherwise. This step helps ensure that your draft has a clear roadmap before you begin the actual writing process.

At this stage, it is essential to refine the AI-generated outputs as much as possible. Challenge its suggestions, revise where necessary, and ensure that the structure aligns with your vision. Do not settle until you are fully comfortable with the organization of your chapters and subchapters (if writing an article) or the overall structure of your academic document. While you can always revisit and adjust later, establishing a clear framework now will save significant time and effort in the long run. The more structured and coherent your work is at this stage, the smoother the writing and revision process will be.

Once you have finalized the structure, you can move on to the next stage: writing. One of the most effective strategies at this point is to simply start—without overthinking. Academic writing often begins as a collection of fragmented ideas, half-formed arguments, or loosely connected points. The key is to get words on the page. You do not need to aim for perfection in your first draft; instead, focus on putting down your thoughts, even if they feel incomplete or unpolished. Instead of waiting for a perfect sentence to emerge, write down whatever comes to mind. Whether it's a rough thesis, an outline, or even just key terms, getting words on the page is the first step. You can do this directly in a generative AI tool or in a standard word processor. When you encounter a roadblock—whether it's struggling to articulate a concept, lacking an example, or feeling uncertain about a transition—use brackets such as "[ ]" to leave a placeholder and insert a short prompt for AI assistance. For instance, you might write:

[Complete this section with an example of X] or **[Refine this paragraph to improve clarity]**. If you have a specific point in mind but are struggling to phrase it effectively, you can provide additional guidance, such as: **[Rewrite this section: What I mean to say is that my proposed theory challenges the conventional understanding of...]**.

At this stage, don't worry about grammatical mistakes or stylistic imperfections—AI will handle them for you. One of the most significant advantages of generative AI is its ability to interpret and refine rough drafts, even when they contain typos, incomplete sentences, or awkward phrasing. As long as you provide sufficient context and substance, the AI will generally comprehend your intended meaning and generate a more polished version of your text. This allows you to focus entirely on your ideas and arguments without being distracted by surface-level refinements. For the first time in academic history, scholars can prioritize content development while delegating the mechanics of language to AI—liberating you from the constant burden of self-editing during the drafting process.

Notably, the writing process will vary from person to person—some may prefer to draft each paragraph independently before using AI for refinement, while others may write in a more fragmented way, using AI to fill in gaps as they go. Both approaches are valid, and the key is to find a method that aligns with your workflow. Some writers might compose entire sections themselves and then use AI to enhance clarity, coherence, or argumentation. Others might write rough drafts interspersed with AI-generated completions, using prompts like "**[Continue this argument with an example]**" or "**[Strengthen this paragraph by incorporating a counterpoint]**." There is no single correct way to use AI in drafting; rather, it is about finding a balance that keeps you engaged while ensuring that AI serves as a helpful collaborator rather than a replacement for your intellectual effort.

As you draft, it is essential to maintain continuity within your AI interactions. Many generative AI tools retain some level of conversational memory, meaning that keeping your writing process within the same session can improve consistency. If you frequently start new conversations, the AI might treat each prompt as an isolated request, lacking context from previous exchanges. This is particularly important when working on a long-term project like a journal article, dissertation, or grant proposal. Some AI tools are gradually improving their ability to remember details across multiple interactions, but for now, it is best to ensure continuity by staying within the same thread whenever possible. That said, be mindful of

AI's limitations—over time, even within the same conversation, it may begin to forget earlier details. When necessary, periodically reintroduce key points to ensure the AI remains aligned with your objectives.

Regardless of which drafting method you choose, the key is to remain **actively critical** of AI-generated content, especially in the early stages. Generative AI does not truly "understand" your topic—it predicts text based on patterns, which means it may produce outputs that are structurally sound but conceptually weak. It might misinterpret your intended style, introduce irrelevant arguments, or generate text that feels generic or superficial. If you do not rigorously evaluate the first few AI-assisted paragraphs, you risk having to make extensive corrections later. Instead, take the time to refine the initial sections carefully, ensuring they align with your argument, style, and intended audience. By setting a high standard from the beginning, you can streamline the drafting process and minimize the need for substantial revisions down the line.

Once you have an initial draft, you can begin fine-tuning both content and style. At this stage, AI is particularly useful in shaping the tone of your writing. Whether you want your text to reflect your established style, emulate a particular academic voice, or balance accessibility with rigor, AI can assist in refining it. Some AI tools allow you to upload sample texts to analyze writing patterns, while others can adjust their output based on direct instructions. For example, you might prompt: "Rewrite this paragraph in a more formal academic tone" or "Make this passage clearer while maintaining a professional style." However, AI will not always get it right on the first try. Refining style requires iteration—if an AI-generated revision does not meet your expectations, provide explicit feedback. Be as detailed as possible, for instance: "This version is too verbose; please condense it while preserving the key argument." Treat the AI as a capable but imprecise assistant—one that requires clear direction and ongoing adjustments to match your expectations.

Another powerful feature of AI-assisted writing is its ability to help refine and structure arguments dynamically. If you feel that a particular section is weak or lacks depth, you can use AI to expand upon it by prompting: "Strengthen this argument by incorporating an additional perspective from [a particular field or scholar]" or "Identify potential objections to this claim and suggest counterarguments." This process can be particularly useful when developing a complex theoretical framework, as AI can help surface ideas that you might not have initially considered. However, it is crucial to remain skeptical—AI-generated expansions may sometimes introduce inaccuracies, misrepresent scholarly debates, or provide arguments that seem plausible but lack proper grounding in academic literature (we will get back to this). Always cross-check AI-generated suggestions against actual sources to ensure that your work remains rigorous and well-supported.

By this stage, you should have a working draft that includes your main arguments, structured sections, and an evolving writing style. However, before moving on to final revisions, it is worth considering how AI can help with **redundancy, clarity, and precision**. Even experienced writers tend to repeat ideas unintentionally or over-explain certain points. AI can assist in streamlining your text by identifying areas where arguments overlap, sentences are unnecessarily complex, or explanations could be more concise. You might prompt: "Identify redundant phrases and suggest a more concise version" or "Simplify this explanation while preserving its accuracy." Some AI tools can also evaluate sentence structure, suggesting ways to improve clarity without sacrificing depth. While these refinements are valuable, they should always be reviewed critically—AI does not always recognize the nuances of emphasis, rhetorical choices, or intentional repetition used for effect. Use it as a tool for improvement, but let your judgment determine what changes to keep.

At this point, you may also want to take advantage of AI tools to simulate a **peer review process** before submitting your work. A useful technique is to prompt AI to act as multiple reviewers, each evaluating your draft from different perspectives. For example, you might ask: "Act as a journal reviewer and critique this paper for publication in [specific journal]. Identify weaknesses and suggest improvements." If the journal has publicly available submission guidelines or reviewer criteria, you can even include these in your prompt for a more tailored critique. This approach can help uncover gaps in argumentation, highlight areas that may need further support, or identify where your claims might be unclear to readers. However, be mindful that AI-generated critiques, while useful, are not a substitute for feedback from real experts in your field. Rather, they should be treated as an additional layer of refinement before seeking input from colleagues or submitting your work for formal peer review.

Once you have revised your draft based on AI-generated feedback, you can take the process a step further by **iterating through multiple review cycles**. A common mistake is assuming that a single AI-assisted review is enough to catch all issues. To avoid this, consider running your draft through AI in different contexts. For example, after addressing one set of critiques, open a new AI conversation and ask it to review the revised draft as if seeing it for the first time. This minimizes bias from the AI's earlier responses and allows for fresh feedback. You can also use different AI models—what one tool overlooks, another might catch. If an earlier review flagged structural weaknesses, the next iteration can focus on clarity, conciseness, or argumentative strength. This layered approach helps refine your text progressively, ensuring that by the final draft, your work is as polished and rigorous as possible.

Beyond critique and refinement, AI can also assist in **fact-checking and verifying sources**. While generative AI is not a substitute for a thorough literature review, it can help identify potential gaps, inconsistencies, or even errors in your citations. If your draft includes claims that need further substantiation, you can prompt AI to suggest relevant sources: "Identify key scholarly articles that discuss [specific topic]" or "Check whether this argument aligns with recent research in [field]." However, it is crucial to be aware that AI models, including those integrated with search functions, may *hallucinate* sources—fabricating plausible-sounding citations that do not actually exist. Always verify references manually by consulting original texts and reputable databases. A best practice is to use AI as a tool to refine your search strategy rather than as a direct source of citations. This ensures academic integrity and prevents reliance on unreliable or non-existent references.

Once your draft is polished and fact-checked, AI can also assist in **enhancing accessibility and engagement**. Academic writing often leans toward complexity, but ensuring clarity—especially for interdisciplinary audiences—is crucial. AI can help by rephrasing dense sections, simplifying explanations, or adjusting the level of technicality based on your intended readership. For example, you might prompt: "Rewrite this paragraph for a broader audience while maintaining academic rigor" or "Explain this concept in a way that a non-expert in my field would understand." This technique is particularly useful when preparing grant proposals, public-facing research summaries, or interdisciplinary work where clarity is key. Additionally, if you need to tailor your writing for different formats—such as turning a journal article into a conference talk or an op-ed—AI can assist in adapting the content while preserving its core arguments.

At this stage, you may also consider using AI for **final proofreading and formatting adjustments**. While AI-assisted grammar and style checks are not infallible, they can quickly identify overlooked typos, awkward phrasing, or inconsistencies in tone. Tools such as ChatGPT, Grammarly, or Claude can highlight structural weaknesses, suggest improvements, and ensure adherence to formal academic writing conventions. You can prompt AI with specific requests, such as "Check this text for grammatical errors and inconsistencies" or "Ensure that this paper follows APA/Chicago/MLA formatting guidelines." This can save valuable time, especially when preparing work for submission to journals with strict formatting requirements. However, as with all AI-generated output, manual oversight is essential. Automated corrections can occasionally misinterpret context or introduce unintended changes, so the final review should always be conducted by the author to maintain precision and authenticity.

Finally, AI can be a powerful tool for **self-evaluation and iterative improvement**. Even after proofreading and formatting, you may want to reassess your work through different perspectives. One effective technique is to use AI to simulate different types of readers—such as journal editors, grant reviewers, or scholars from adjacent disciplines. You can prompt: "Evaluate this introduction from the perspective of a grant reviewer assessing its clarity and significance" or "Analyze this argument as if you were a peer reviewer looking for logical weaknesses." By engaging in multiple rounds of AI-assisted self-evaluation, you can preemptively address issues that might otherwise be flagged during the formal review process. This iterative approach ensures that your final submission is not just polished in terms of language and formatting but also intellectually rigorous, well-structured, and strategically positioned for your intended audience.

These are merely examples of how to engage with generative AI tools in writing. As you gain more experience, you will develop your own methods for utilizing these tools as an effective thinking and writing assistant. With the emergence of AI models specifically tailored for academic writing, these capabilities are likely to become even more sophisticated, offering enhanced support in structuring arguments, refining prose, and adapting to disciplinary conventions.

It is also worth mentioning here—though we will explore this in greater depth in another chapter—that once your draft is complete, it is advisable to check for plagiarism before submission. Generally, plagiarism should not be a major concern when generative AI is used correctly, as these models generate text rather than copying verbatim from existing sources. However, the risk increases when using AI tools that retrieve and summarize external content. If an AI model pulls directly from an online article or database, its output may closely resemble the original material, raising concerns about improper attribution.

To ensure originality, plagiarism detection software can be used. Some widely available tools include Grammarly's plagiarism checker, Turnitin—commonly used in academic institutions—and iThenticate, which is specifically designed for researchers and journal submissions. Many of these services require institutional access or paid subscriptions, so it is worth checking whether your university or organization provides access before purchasing a license. Taking these precautions helps maintain academic integrity and ensures that AI-assisted writing remains aligned with ethical and professional standards.

Obviously, other important ethical considerations arise when using AI in academic writing. While AI-generated text itself does not constitute plagiarism, relying on AI to paraphrase without proper citation can be ethically problematic. If AI assists in summarizing or restructuring an argument derived from an existing source, the original work should still be credited. Treating AI as a writing assistant rather than a replacement for proper research and citation practices is essential for maintaining academic integrity. These ethical concerns, along with broader implications of AI use in academia, will be explored in greater detail later in this book.

In sum, the drafting process with generative AI is not about replacing human intellectual effort but about enhancing efficiency, overcoming writer's block, and refining academic writing. By treating AI as an engaged collaborator rather than a passive content generator, scholars can leverage its capabilities to structure ideas, critique arguments, and streamline their writing workflows. However, critical oversight remains essential at every stage—whether in verifying AI-generated content, refining its stylistic suggestions, or ensuring that originality and academic integrity are upheld. With a well-structured draft in place, the next steps involve managing citations and references, where AI can assist in formatting bibliographies and cross-checking sources while avoiding the pitfalls of hallucinated citations. Additionally, AI can play a role in optimizing publication strategies by aligning manuscripts with journal requirements, crafting submission materials, and adapting research for different audiences. As we move into these aspects of writing and publishing with AI, the focus remains on integrating these tools responsibly, ensuring they serve as aids rather than substitutes for scholarly expertise.

CITATIONS AND REFERENCES

Citing sources has become significantly easier with AI-powered tools. Long before the advent of generative AI, citation management software like Zotero, EndNote, and Mendeley simplified the process of organizing references and formatting citations correctly. These tools remain valuable today and are gradually integrating generative AI capabilities to enhance their functionality. Generative AI models like ChatGPT and Claude can already assist in formatting citations, managing bibliographies, and even cross-checking references. With proper guidance, AI can quickly format citations according to APA, Chicago, MLA, Bluebook, or any other required style, significantly reducing the time and effort required for citation management. However, while AI can streamline citation tasks, its outputs should always be reviewed manually, as occasional errors—such as incorrect formatting, missing details, or inconsistencies—can still occur.

AI, however, is not inherently reliable when generating citations from scratch. One of the most critical issues is the previously mentioned AI hallucinations—when a model fabricates sources, inventing author names, journal titles, publication years, and even page numbers. If you ask AI to provide references without supplying the correct data, it may create citations that appear legitimate but are entirely fictional. To avoid this, always locate and verify the original source before using AI to format citations. Rather than asking AI to cite sources on a given topic, provide it with actual references. Many AI tools now allow you to upload source materials directly, enabling them to extract the correct bibliographic details. Once the information is verified, you can use AI to format citations in the required style—whether APA, Chicago, MLA, Bluebook, or another. Additionally, AI can help check a list of citations for consistency, ensuring uniformity in formatting. However, always review the AI-generated output carefully, as it may still contain minor formatting inconsistencies. If errors occur, correct them and guide the AI to ensure that future citations align with your preferred style.

AI is also useful for managing entire bibliographies. If you have a list of references, you can instruct AI to alphabetize it, arrange it by publication year, or standardize formatting across different citation styles. This can be particularly helpful when merging references from multiple sources, ensuring consistency and adherence to specific style guidelines. Additionally, AI can assist in detecting missing details, such as incomplete author names or missing page numbers, and suggest corrections. However, as with all AI-generated content, the final bibliography should always be reviewed manually. AI may occasionally omit crucial information, misorder entries, or misinterpret subtle distinctions between citation styles. While these tools can significantly streamline the process, human oversight remains essential to ensure accuracy and compliance with academic standards.

For book authors or those working on extensive research projects requiring an index, AI can also be a valuable tool. Manually compiling an index is a time-consuming and meticulous task, but AI can assist in generating a preliminary draft. By uploading a manuscript, you can prompt AI to identify key terms, extract significant names and concepts, or organize references based on specific themes or categories. This can provide a useful starting point, saving time in the indexing process. However, as with citations, indexing requires careful verification. AI may misassign page numbers, overlook crucial terms, or fail to prioritize the most relevant concepts. Additionally, it might generate an index that is too broad or insufficiently structured for specialized academic work. Therefore, any AI-generated index should be treated as a rough draft, to be refined manually to ensure accuracy, coherence, and relevance to the text.

The key takeaway here is to find the right balance between using AI to automate time-consuming (and often tedious) tasks and ensuring that it does not introduce errors that compromise your work. AI can significantly free up time for the more intellectually demanding and creative aspects of research and writing, but it requires careful calibration. Finding this balance is often a process of trial and error—adjusting how you integrate AI into your workflow until it aligns with your specific needs. Once the AI is fine-tuned to your preferences, the process will become more seamless. While human oversight remains essential (as we have repeatedly emphasized due to its critical importance), AI can still play a valuable role in streamlining your academic work.

PUBLICATION OPTIMIZATION

If you are preparing an article, the next logical step after writing is publishing. AI should not replace your institutional or personal preferences regarding where to submit your work. Choosing the right journal or publisher depends on various factors, including where you want your research to be seen, the impact factor of the journal, and the relevance of your work to its readership. While AI can assist in gathering information about potential publication venues, it is still advisable to consult with peers, mentors, or colleagues who are familiar with the publishing landscape in your field.

Once you have identified your target journal or publisher, AI can help optimize your submission strategy. Many journals have specific formatting and stylistic requirements, and AI can assist in ensuring that your manuscript aligns with these guidelines. You can upload the journal's submission requirements and ask AI to check whether your document follows them correctly, adjusting elements such as citation style, word count, and section headings accordingly. If you are unsure whether your work fits within the journal's scope, you can also upload abstracts or introductions from recent issues to analyze patterns in style, methodology, or framing. This can provide useful insights into how to refine your manuscript to better align with the journal's expectations.

AI can also assist with crafting submission materials, such as cover letters or abstracts. Many journals require a cover letter explaining the significance of the research and why it is a good fit for their publication. Instead of drafting this from scratch, you can provide AI with key details—such as the research question, main contributions, and journal name—and ask it to generate a draft. While AI-generated letters should always be reviewed and personalized, they can save time by providing a structured starting point. Similarly, AI can help refine abstracts to ensure they are clear, concise, and engaging, aligning with the journal's preferred style.

For those submitting to multiple journals, AI can be useful in adapting an article for different audiences. Journals often have varying scopes, requiring authors to adjust emphasis or framing to match the readership. AI can help with this process by suggesting how to reposition arguments or modify language to fit different editorial priorities. However, as with all AI-assisted processes, human oversight is essential—an AI may suggest changes that do not fully align with the paper's core arguments or misinterpret disciplinary conventions.

Beyond journal articles, AI can also assist with optimizing book proposals, conference submissions, and research summaries for broader dissemination. Whether preparing an article for an open-access platform, adjusting a manuscript for a different discipline, or summarizing findings for a general audience, AI can help streamline the adaptation process while ensuring consistency in messaging.

CONCLUSION

Generative AI is reshaping academic writing and publishing, enhancing productivity and streamlining workflows. From brainstorming and structuring arguments to refining drafts, formatting citations, and optimizing submissions, AI serves as a valuable collaborator in scholarly communication. However, it does not replace critical thinking, originality, or methodological rigor—scholars must balance AI's efficiencies with human oversight to maintain academic integrity. While AI can assist in citation management, indexing, and manuscript optimization, its outputs require careful scrutiny. Risks such as hallucinated citations, shallow engagement with literature, and the homogenization of discourse must be actively mitigated. Transparency in AI usage is increasingly required by institutions and publishers, making responsible disclosure essential.

Looking ahead, AI's role in academia will continue to evolve, raising new questions about authorship, attribution, and intellectual labor. The challenge is not whether to use AI, but how to integrate it responsibly. By leveraging AI's strengths while ensuring intellectual rigor, scholars can enhance efficiency without compromising the depth and originality of their work.

REFERENCES

Barros, A., Prasad, A., & Śliwa, M. (2023). Generative artificial intelligence and academia: Implications for research, teaching, and service. *Management Learning, 54*(5), 597–604. https://doi.org/10.1177/13505076231201445

Cotton, D. R. E., Cotton, P. A., & Shipway, J. R. (2024). Chatting and cheating: Ensuring academic integrity in the era of ChatGPT. *Innovations in Education and Teaching International, 61*(2), 228–239. https://doi.org/10.108 0/14703297.2023.2190148

Dwivedi, Y. K., Kshetri, N., Hughes, L., Slade, E. L., Simintiras, A. C., Kar, A. K., & Baabdullah, A. M. (2023). 'So What If ChatGPT Wrote It?' Multidisciplinary perspectives on opportunities, challenges, and implications of generative conversational AI for research, practice, and policy. *International Journal of Information Management, 71*, 102642.

Grimes, M., von Krogh, G., Feuerriegel, S., Rink, F., & Gruber, M. (2023). From scarcity to abundance: Scholars and scholarship in an age of generative artificial intelligence. *Academy of Management Journal, 66*(6), 1617–1624. https://doi.org/10.5465/amj.2023.4006

Holmes, W. (2023). The unintended consequences of artificial intelligence and education. *Education International*. https://www.ei-ie.org/en/item/28115: the-unintended-consequences-of-artificial-intelligence-and-education

Kulkarni, M., Mantere, S., Vaara, E., van den Broek, E., Pachidi, S., Glaser, V. L., Gehman, J., Petriglieri, G., Lindebaum, D., Cameron, L. D., Rahman, H. A., Islam, G., & Greenwood, M. (2024). The future of research in an artificial intelligence-driven world. *Journal of Management Inquiry, 33*(3), 207–229.

Milano, S., McGrane, J. A., & Leonelli, S. (2023). Large language models challenge the future of higher education. *Nature Machine Intelligence, 5*(4), 333–334.

Stokel-Walker, C. (2023). ChatGPT listed as author on research papers: Many scientists disapprove. *Nature*. https://www.nature.com/articles/d41586-023-00107-z

Wagner, G., Lukyanenko, R., & Paré, G. (2022). Artificial intelligence and the conduct of literature reviews. *Journal of Information Technology, 37*(2), 209–226.

CHAPTER 5

AI in Data Management and Analysis

Abstract This chapter explores how AI is revolutionizing academic data management and analysis by automating labor-intensive tasks such as data wrangling, cleaning, integration, and exploratory analysis. From structured survey data to unstructured textual content, generative AI and machine learning tools can detect anomalies, suggest harmonizations, engineer new features, and reveal patterns at scale. The chapter offers practical insights into tools like Google DataPrep, Airtable, and Wikidata, while emphasizing the continued need for human oversight. It cautions against over-reliance on automated suggestions and underscores the importance of validation, reproducibility, and ethical data governance in AI-assisted research workflows.

Keywords Data cleaning • AI in research • Data integration • Exploratory analysis • Feature engineering

Contemporary academic research has been fundamentally reshaped by the unprecedented scale and complexity of available data (Kitchin, 2014; Boyd & Crawford, 2012). Nearly all fields of academia are becoming datafied (Flensburg & Lomborg, 2021): datafication is the new buzzword, and the data become the new coin of the academic realm.

© The Author(s), under exclusive license to Springer Nature
Switzerland AG 2025
E. Haber et al., *Using AI in Academic Writing and Research*,
https://doi.org/10.1007/978-3-031-91705-9_5

After researchers obtain their datasets—through traditional collection, computational methods, or automated systems—they encounter significant challenges in preparing, integrating, and conducting preliminary analyses of their data. These preparatory phases demand considerable expertise and resources while potentially introducing vulnerabilities through systematic errors, biases, or inefficiencies in research procedures (Kaisler et al., 2013; Jagadish et al., 2014).

In response to these challenges, artificial intelligence technologies, especially machine learning and natural language processing, have become instrumental in research data management. These systems now support dataset structuring, detect anomalies at scale, and reveal promising analytical pathways (Jordan & Mitchell, 2015; LeCun et al., 2015). By reducing the time spent on routine data preparation, researchers can dedicate more attention to sophisticated analysis and theoretical interpretation, enhancing their work's efficiency and quality.

The benefits of incorporating artificial intelligence in research extend beyond improved efficiency. Systems trained on extensive datasets excel at classifying unstructured information, revealing hidden patterns, and identifying subtle inconsistencies that traditional methods might miss (Chen et al., 2012; Wu et al., 2014). This capability proves particularly valuable in modern academic research, where datasets range from historical documents to real-time digital information streams.

The implementation of these technologies in research requires careful consideration and planning. Researchers must ensure alignment between their data characteristics, methodological approaches, and chosen technological solutions. Particular attention must be given to maintaining transparency, reproducibility, and ethical data governance (Kitchin, 2014; Mittelstadt & Floridi, 2016). When properly implemented, these advanced data management approaches can substantially improve research quality while facilitating the transition from raw information to meaningful scientific understanding. This chapter will look into how to harness these tools to our advantage.

AI-Assisted Data Wrangling and Cleaning

Data wrangling and cleaning is one of the most resource-intensive stages of research (incidentally, also one of the most boring!), requiring scholars to tackle various issues—from inconsistent file formats to incomplete or erroneous entries (Kandel et al., 2011). Even minor oversights can undermine the validity of subsequent analyses (Zhu & Wu, 2014). With today's datasets spanning spreadsheets, databases, and social media feeds, manually standardizing labels or sifting through thousands of rows for anomalies can be overwhelming. Researchers increasingly use AI-driven techniques for time savings and more reliable error detection and correction.

Many open-source and commercial tools demonstrate how AI can automate or semi-automate tasks such as deduplication, missing data imputation, and anomaly detection (Hellerstein et al., 2017). For instance, Trifacta Wrangler (currently rebranded as Alteryx Designer Cloud)—rooted initially in the research by Kandel and colleagues—applies machine learning to recommend data transformations, while OpenRefine can suggest potential merges for inconsistent string values (e.g., "U.S.A." vs. "United States") by analyzing their similarity. In Python, packages like pandas-profiling or great-expectations generate reports highlighting potential data quality issues, letting researchers rapidly spot irregular distributions or mislabeled columns before those flaws distort their analyses.

One key benefit of AI-assisted tools is their capacity to learn from user feedback and refine their suggestions. Suppose you upload a large spreadsheet to Trifacta Wrangler or run a cleaning script in OpenRefine, or rely on Google DataPrep, and you manually adjust certain text fields—such as unifying "Not applicable," "N/A," and blanks under a single code. Once you confirm these changes, the tool can apply them automatically across your dataset, drastically cutting down repetitive rule-setting (Ebraker & Hellerstein, 2005). This adaptive process is particularly valuable in live data environments, where periodic refreshes may introduce new anomalies that need consistent handling.

Consider a scenario where you merge datasets from several universities to compare graduation rates. One institution labels incomplete records "WD," another "Withdrawn," and another "Drop." An AI-enabled platform might cluster these terms based on semantic similarity and then prompt you to accept or rename them collectively as "Withdrawn." Approving that prompt triggers automated uniformity across all relevant fields. Similarly, in a study of faculty workload, you might use pandas-profiling in Python to detect that one university's numeric "Hours_Taught" column contains outliers—like the suspicious figure of "2,000 hours"—which indicates an error in data entry or unit labeling. Flagging these anomalies early helps researchers correct them before any impact on later modeling.

Beyond structured data, AI-driven solutions also facilitate the cleaning of unstructured data such as interview transcripts or open-ended survey responses (Klinkenberg, 2017). Tools like NLP-based text processors in Python (for example, spaCy or NLTK) can remove boilerplate text, redundant disclaimers, or date stamps, allowing a researcher to concentrate on participant narratives. In large-scale qualitative projects, you might feed PDF documents into an AI-powered pipeline that automatically filters out repeated administrative headers or unrelated legal disclaimers. This ensures you are left with the core textual content for coding and thematic analysis. These workflows streamline data preparation while reducing human errors introduced by manual text parsing.

Ultimately, harnessing AI for data wrangling and cleaning not only expedites the research workflow but also boosts the quality and reliability of subsequent findings. By minimizing repetitive or manual tasks, researchers can focus on applying their subject expertise—interrogating anomalies, refining research questions, and shaping robust interpretations. Still, each AI-driven transformation should be thoroughly documented, with detailed logs of accepted suggestions and rule mappings, to uphold transparency and reproducibility. When balanced with human oversight and careful validation, AI-assisted data cleaning paves the way for more confident data exploration and advanced modeling, setting a solid foundation for meaningful scientific contributions.

Practical Example: Cleaning Customer Survey Responses with Google DataPrep

1. Setup and Data Import

   Access Google DataPrep
   In your Google Cloud Console, navigate to the "Dataprep" section (often listed under "Big Data" or "Data Analytics").
   If this is your first time, create a new **DataPrep flow** or project by following the on-screen instructions to connect to your Google Cloud Storage (GCS) bucket.
   Upload or Connect to Your Dataset
   Place your raw files (e.g., CSV, Excel, or JSON) into a Google Cloud Storage bucket.
   In DataPrep, click **"Import Datasets"**, then select your source. The tool will generate a preview and automatically sample the data.
   Initial Data Assessment

(*continued*)

(continued)

DataPrep automatically generates a **data quality overview**, highlighting issues like missing values or type mismatches.

Explore each column's **profile** (distribution, min/max values) to spot potential errors (e.g., unexpected symbols, out-of-range values).

2. Text Standardization

Locate and Select Free-Text Columns

Identify columns like "Customer_Comments" or "Feedback_Text."

Click on a column header to access transformation options.

Use Built-In "Text Cleanup" Functions

Trim Whitespace: Removes leading/trailing spaces.

Standardize Case: Convert text to lowercase or uppercase for consistency.

Fix Spelling Errors: DataPrep's AI suggestions can automatically correct common typos (e.g., "Smrtphone" → "Smartphone").

Split or Merge Columns (if needed): For example, if city and state are combined into one field, you can split them into two columns.

Preview Changes

DataPrep shows **before-and-after snapshots** of your data each time you apply a transformation. Confirm it looks correct before finalizing.

3. Smart Value Grouping for Categorical Fields

Handle Inconsistent Labels

For categories like "Product_Category," DataPrep can group synonymous or near-duplicate values.

Click the column header and select **"Group Similar Values."**

Approve or Refine Groupings

DataPrep will suggest merges for values like "Smart Phone," "smartphone," and "SmarPhone."

Manually adjust or reject suggestions if they incorrectly bundle distinct values (e.g., "Smartphone" vs. "Smartwatch").

(*continued*)

(continued)
Create Consistent Category Names
Once approved, the tool applies the updated labels throughout the column, ensuring uniform categories across the dataset.

4. Automated Data Quality Checks

Run the "Data Health" Scan
This scan identifies anomalies such as out-of-range rating scores (e.g., "12" in a 1–10 rating) or invalid email formats.
You'll see flagged issues in a sidebar or error summary.
Review and Apply Suggested Fixes
Standardize Rating Scores: If a rating is "12," you might choose to set it to "10" or mark it as invalid.
Correct Date Formats: DataPrep can parse mixed date formats (e.g., "MM/DD/YYYY" vs. "DD/MM/YYYY") and convert them into a single standardized pattern.
Repair Invalid Emails: The tool can remove or fix domain typos like "@gamil.com."
Mark Persistent Issues as Exceptions
If some flagged entries are actually valid edge cases, mark them as acceptable rather than errors.

5. Data Enrichment and Validation

Derived Columns
Create new columns using existing fields (e.g., calculating an "Age Group" based on date of birth).
Add rules to handle borderline cases (e.g., if the date of birth is before 1900, mark as "Potential Error").
Postal Code Validation
For demographic data, enable region-specific checks (e.g., US ZIP codes vs. Canadian postal codes).
DataPrep can highlight mismatches, prompting you to fix or remove invalid records.
Temporal Consistency
Standardize the date/time columns into ISO 8601 (YYYY-MM-DD HH:MM:SS) or another consistent format.

(continued)

(continued)

If your dataset has multiple timestamp columns (e.g., "Response_Submit_Time" and "Survey_Start_Time"), ensure they use the same time zone offset.

6. Creating a Reusable Recipe and Exporting

   Save Transformations as a Recipe

   Every step—splitting columns, grouping values, or correcting data types—is automatically logged in a "recipe."

   Name and version your recipe for future reuse or collaboration.

   Preview Your Cleaned Dataset

   Use the sample view to confirm all transformations look correct.

   Verify record counts, column names, and any derived fields.

   Export Options

   Output the cleaned data as **CSV, Excel**, or send it directly to a **database** or **BigQuery** table.

   Retain the recipe so that future runs can be applied to updated datasets with minimal additional effort.

   Why Use Google DataPrep?

   Integration with Google Cloud: Effortlessly connect to Cloud Storage or BigQuery for scalable data processing.

   AI-Powered Suggestions: Smart transformations reduce guesswork, letting you focus on domain-specific decision-making.

   Audit Trail & Version Control: All transformations are recorded, fostering reproducibility and facilitating peer review.

   Large Dataset Handling: DataPrep can handle millions of rows without relying on local machine memory, which is essential for enterprise-level or longitudinal studies.

DATA INTEGRATION AND HARMONIZATION

In contemporary research, data are rarely sourced from a single repository or generated by a solitary instrument. Rather, they often emanate from disparate databases, APIs, archived reports, and real-time feeds, each with its own structure and semantics (Kitchin, 2014). Integrating these heterogeneous sources into a unified dataset—so that analyses can capture the full scope of a phenomenon—requires a careful process of matching, mapping, and harmonizing disparate fields (Verborgh et al., 2016). AI, combined with user-friendly platforms, can streamline this task by automatically detecting relationships between datasets and suggesting how best to merge, align, or reconcile conflicting schema elements.

While coding and scripting skills have traditionally been a barrier to complex data integration, a growing number of **no-code** or **low-code** tools are making these capabilities more accessible (Ciechanowski et al., 2020). Platforms such as **Zapier, Make (formerly Integromat)**, and **Airtable** allow researchers to connect different services—like Google Sheets, SQL databases, and even web APIs—through intuitive drag-and-drop interfaces. These tools often incorporate AI-driven recommendations for mapping and merging fields; for example, they might suggest joining two tables on similar column names or prompt the user to align date formats across data sources. When used carefully, these automated suggestions can reduce integration time dramatically.

As data integration and harmonization become simpler through no-code or low-code platforms, researchers can devote more attention to interpreting results and designing subsequent analyses rather than getting bogged down in manual merges and transformations. Still, it remains vital to validate automated suggestions, maintain version control of merged datasets, and keep detailed documentation to preserve transparency (Kaisler et al., 2013). When implemented thoughtfully, AI-powered integration workflows reduce errors, expedite time-to-insight, and empower multidisciplinary teams to combine and reconcile diverse data sources more effectively.

Practical Example

Imagine you have an online survey in **Typeform** collecting free-text responses and a second source—a CSV export from your institutional demographic records. A platform like **Zapier** can ingest new survey responses, check for matching email addresses in the CSV, and merge data into a single table in **Airtable**. Researchers can further leverage AI-driven suggestions within Airtable's "Automations" feature to unify inconsistent demographic labels or correct truncated addresses before saving the updated records.

If you frequently receive multiple Excel files from different collaborators, you can use **Make** to watch a shared folder in Google Drive, ingest each incoming file, and append its rows to a

(*continued*)

(continued)
master dataset (e.g., in Google BigQuery). The system flags any new columns or unexpected value types, prompting you to decide how they should be integrated.

Sometimes, your project includes textual interview transcripts plus numeric survey data. Tools like **Power Automate** (part of Microsoft Power Platform) can orchestrate dataflows where an AI-driven text-analysis step (e.g., Azure Cognitive Services for entity recognition) runs on the transcripts. The processed outputs—like sentiment scores or topic labels—are appended to a central dataset that also includes each participant's survey responses. This approach simplifies correlation analyses between open-ended comments and structured ratings.

If you have multiple datasets labeling the same variable differently—say "SatisfactionScore," "User_Sat," and "Sat_Score"—AI-driven suggestions in a tool like **Airtable** or **OpenRefine** can propose a consistent, harmonized field name. You simply approve the recommendation, and the platform applies the change across all records, significantly reducing manual overhead.

Researchers may also tap into external data sources, such as a social media platform's API or a weather data feed. Using a no-code integration tool, you configure an endpoint to fetch JSON or XML data, then let AI-driven mapping features recommend how to align the incoming fields with your existing database columns. The system might detect that "temp_f" from the weather feed should match your "Temperature_Fahrenheit" column, or that "user_screen_name" from X's API maps to "TwitterHandle." Confirming or adjusting these mappings ensures consistent naming and data types across your integrated dataset.

Exploratory Analysis and Feature Engineering with AI

Exploratory Data Analysis (EDA) aims to reveal underlying patterns, anomalies, and relationships before formal modeling commences (Tukey, 1977). Traditionally, researchers sift through plots and summary statistics by hand, but today's extensive datasets make this a daunting task (Han et al., 2012). AI-based tools can automate much of the heavy lifting, suggesting important correlations and highlighting distributions of interest. For example, imagine a dataset of 10,000 student records from different schools around the country: a no-code platform such as **Tableau Prep** can ingest your CSV file, automatically generate histograms for each variable, and highlight outliers in attendance rates. Simultaneously, a **ChatGPT** workflow could generate high-level summaries ("Attendance is highly correlated with final exam scores, especially in lower-income districts"), sparing you from manual scanning of hundreds of pivot tables.

One benefit of these AI-driven EDA platforms is that they can handle tasks like correlation analysis, clustering, and dimensionality reduction with little to no coding (Witten et al., 2011). For instance, a researcher studying climate data might upload time-series files into **DataRobot's** no-code interface, automatically generating correlation heatmaps and scatterplots for variables such as temperature, humidity, and pollution levels. With just a few clicks, you can see that humidity levels spike in tandem with specific pollution indicators—insights that might not be obvious until an automated workflow points them out. Afterward, you can fine-tune these revelations using advanced queries in a user-friendly environment rather than scripting everything from scratch.

Moving on to feature engineering, researchers frequently develop new variables—either by combining existing columns or extracting meaningful signals from raw data—to boost model performance and interpretability (Kuhn & Johnson, 2013). In a marketing scenario, you might have customer purchase logs that contain timestamps. Using a visual tool like **Airtable** with AI-powered extensions, you could create a "TimeSinceLastPurchase" column or derive a "Morning vs. Evening" purchase feature simply by clicking through a guided workflow. If you need text transformations—for example, turning free-text product reviews into sentiment scores—a quick prompt to **ChatGPT** might produce regex or pseudo-code examples that you can adapt directly into your no-code environment.

Automated feature engineering can go further by algorithmically suggesting transformations, binning numeric values, or creating interaction variables (Chandrashekar & Sahin, 2014). Suppose you're studying a public health dataset with daily step counts, body mass index (BMI), and hours of sleep. A platform like **H2O Driverless AI** can offer transformations—such as "average steps over past 7 days" or "BMI category multiplied by average sleep hours"—which might boost predictive power for specific health outcomes. Even if you're not confident in advanced statistics, these recommendations let you experiment with new variables quickly and see immediate feedback on how they influence a model's accuracy or explanatory power.

Another real-life use case involves working with textual and numerical data in tandem. Imagine you've collected open-ended survey responses about product satisfaction alongside star ratings. A tool like **MonkeyLearn** can generate a sentiment analysis score for each comment, while your no-code dashboard—say, **Power BI**—automatically merges these scores with the numeric ratings in a single table for exploratory correlation. You might discover that low star ratings often contradict surprisingly positive textual sentiments, prompting further investigation into survey design or user experience. This synergy of AI-based EDA and feature engineering ensures that even non-programmers can uncover multifaceted insights rapidly (Witten et al., 2011).

It is worth mentioning that Google Sheets offers many data clean-up tools by default, and there are plenty of add-ons doing additional analyses, including sentiment analysis. However, it is often difficult to pull on a larger dataset. One notable and helpful add-on for Google Sheets is Wikipedia and Wikidata Tools, allowing querying Wikimedia databases from within the spreadsheet.

Using Wikimedia data is immensely useful for exploratory data analysis in itself. Large, collaboratively maintained free and open knowledge graphs such as **Wikidata** allow amazing quick-and-not-so-dirty studies and visualizations (Turki et al., 2021, 2022). Wikidata contains structured, linked data on millions of entities—people, places, concepts, and more—making it ideal for supplementing an existing dataset with additional context or relationships. For example, a researcher examining the geographic distribution of Nobel laureates might query Wikidata to retrieve standardized metadata on each laureate's country of birth, academic affiliation, or fields of study. They can then merge these details into a no-code analysis platform like **Tableau** or **Power BI** for further visualization. Wikidata and Wikipedia can allow for fun studies, too: one of us discovered that Olympic medalists live shorter than non-medalist Olympic sportspeople (Kovbasiuk et al., 2024) by tapping into the Wikimedia free resources.

Tools like the **Wikidata Query Service** (which uses SPARQL) provide a user-friendly interface for retrieving specific slices of linked data. At the same time, Python wrappers (e.g., **wikidata2df**) can automate these queries for repeatable workflows. This seamless integration of open knowledge resources can reveal hidden connections—like shared universities or overlapping research topics—that might otherwise be missed in local datasets, enhancing the depth and breadth of an exploratory analysis.

Despite these advantages, caution is crucial. Automated workflows can propose large numbers of new variables, some of which may reflect transient or spurious patterns rather than true signals (Friedman, 2001). When you discover an unexpected association—like an oddly strong correlation between "Average Customer Ticket Size" and "Browser Language"—it's prudent to validate it against domain knowledge and potentially cross-validate results with a more rigorous manual check. By combining the efficiency of AI-driven EDA and feature engineering with informed scholarly judgment, researchers can accelerate discovery while reducing the risk of chasing noise. In essence, AI tools do not replace human insight; they empower it, allowing researchers to spend more energy on conceptual breakthroughs and less on repetitive data tasks.

CONCLUSION

AI is fundamentally transforming data management and analysis, enabling researchers to efficiently handle increasingly large, complex, and heterogeneous datasets. By automating tedious yet critical tasks—such as data wrangling, cleaning, integration, and exploratory analysis—AI-driven tools significantly enhance research productivity, accuracy, and reproducibility. These technologies empower scholars to rapidly uncover hidden patterns, correct errors, harmonize disparate sources, and engineer insightful new features, facilitating deeper and more nuanced analyses. However, the promise of AI-driven data management must always be balanced by rigorous validation, ethical considerations, and transparent documentation. While AI streamlines workflows and identifies valuable insights, human judgment remains crucial in verifying automated suggestions, preventing the propagation of systematic biases, and ensuring the validity of scientific conclusions. Ultimately, AI does not replace scholarly expertise but significantly augments it, freeing researchers from mundane tasks to engage more deeply with their data, fostering innovative discoveries, and enhancing the overall rigor of academic research.

References

Boyd, D., & Crawford, K. (2012). Critical questions for Big Data: Provocations for a cultural, technological, and scholarly phenomenon. *Information, Communication & Society, 15*(5), 662–679.

Chandrashekar, G., & Sahin, F. (2014). A survey on feature selection methods. *Computers & Electrical Engineering: An International Journal, 40*(1), 16–28.

Chen, H., Chiang, R. H. L., & Storey, V. C. (2012). Business intelligence and analytics: From Big Data to big impact. *MIS Quarterly: Management Information Systems, 36*(4), 1165.

Ciechanowski, L., Jemielniak, D., & Gloor, P. A. (2020). AI research without coding: The art of fighting without fighting: Data science for qualitative researchers. *Journal of Business Research, 117*(September), 322–330.

Ebraker, M., & Hellerstein, J. M. (2005). What goes around comes around. In *Readings in database systems* (pp. 35–60). MIT Press.

Flensburg, S., & Lomborg, S. (2021). Datafication research: Mapping the field for a future agenda. *New Media & Society*, (September), 146144482110466.

Friedman, J. H. (2001). The role of variable selection in statistical learning. In *Proceedings of the 20th international workshop on machine learning* (pp. 85–94). Morgan Kaufmann.

Han, J., Kamber, M., & Pei, J. (2012). *Data mining: Concepts and techniques* (The Morgan Kaufmann series in data management systems). Morgan Kaufmann.

Hellerstein, J. M., Stein, L. A., Heer, J., & Kandel, S. (2017). Data wrangling: Techniques and best practices for data preparation. *Communications of the ACM, 60*(9), 56–65.

Jagadish, H. V., Gehrke, J., Labrinidis, A., Papakonstantinou, Y., Patel, J. M., Ramakrishnan, R., & Shahabi, C. (2014). Big Data and its technical challenges. *Communications of the ACM, 57*(7), 86–94.

Jordan, M. I., & Mitchell, T. M. (2015). Machine learning: Trends, perspectives, and prospects. *Science (New York, N.Y.), 349*(6245), 255–260.

Kaisler, S., Frank, A., Alberto Espinosa, J., & Money, W. (2013). Big Data: Issues and challenges moving forward. In *2013 46th Hawaii international conference on system sciences*. IEEE. https://doi.org/10.1109/hicss.2013.645

Kandel, S., Heer, J., Plaisant, C., Kennedy, J., van Ham, F., Riche, N. H., Weaver, C., Lee, B., Brodbeck, D., & Buono, P. (2011). Research directions in data wrangling: Visualizations and transformations for usable and credible data. *Information Visualization, 10*(4), 271–288.

Kitchin, R. (2014). *The data revolution: Big Data, open data, data infrastructures and their consequences*. SAGE.

Klinkenberg, R. (2017). Rapid prototyping of data mining solutions for real-world applications. In *Data mining and knowledge discovery handbook* (pp. 131–155). Springer.

Kovbasiuk, A., Ciechanowski, L., & Jemielniak, D. (2024). A taste of ambrosia: Do olympic medalists live longer than Olympic losers? *Scandinavian Journal of Public Health*, (January), 14034948231219833.

Kuhn, M., & Johnson, K. (2013). *Applied predictive modeling* (1st ed.). Springer.

LeCun, Y., Bengio, Y., & Hinton, G. (2015). Deep learning. *Nature, 521*(7553), 436–444.

Mittelstadt, B. D., & Floridi, L. (2016). The ethics of Big Data: Current and foreseeable issues in biomedical contexts. *Science and Engineering Ethics, 22*(2), 303–341.

Tukey, J. W. (1977). *Exploratory data analysis* (Addison-Wesley series in behavioral science. Quantitative methods). Pearson.

Turki, H., Jemielniak, D., Hadj, M. A., Taieb, J. E., Gayo, L., Aouicha, M. B., Banat, M.'a., Shafee, T., et al. (2022). Using logical constraints to validate statistical information about disease outbreaks in collaborative knowledge graphs: The case of COVID-19 epidemiology in Wikidata. *PeerJ Computer Science, 8*(September), e1085.

Turki, H., Taieb, M. A. H., Shafee, T., Lubiana, T., Jemielniak, D., Aouicha, M. B., Gayo, J. E. L., et al. (2021). Representing COVID-19 information in collaborative knowledge graphs: The case of Wikidata. *Semantic Web*, 1–32.

Verborgh, R., Ghaem Sigarchian, H., Troncy, R., & Harth, A. (2016). Managing heterogeneous data sources in a data-driven environment. *IEEE Internet Computing, 20*(2), 34–40.

Witten, I. H., Frank, E., & Hall, M. A. (2011). *Data mining: Practical machine learning tools and techniques* (Morgan Kaufmann series in data management) (3rd ed.). Morgan Kaufmann.

Wu, X., Zhu, X., Wu, G.-Q., & Ding, W. (2014). Data mining with Big Data. *IEEE Transactions on Knowledge and Data Engineering, 26*(1), 97–107.

Zhu, X., & Wu, X. (2014). Class noise vs. attribute noise: A quantitative study of their impacts. *Artificial Intelligence Review, 22*, 177–210.

CHAPTER 6

Presentations

Abstract This chapter explores how generative AI is transforming academic presentations, offering tools that streamline slide creation, tailor content for diverse audiences, and enhance engagement through compelling visuals and adaptive formats. From structuring research talks and simplifying technical explanations to creating customized versions for policymakers, peers, and the public, AI enhances the clarity and accessibility of scholarly communication. The chapter provides practical workflows and tools for literature reviews, statistical methods, and visual storytelling. It also examines emerging trends—such as 3D visualizations, AR/VR, and holographic presentations—alongside best practices for design, social media dissemination, and collaborative workflow integration. While AI accelerates and enriches the presentation process, human oversight remains essential to ensure rigor, accuracy, and credibility.

Keywords AI presentations • Academic communication • Visual storytelling • Research dissemination • Scholarly engagement

Presentations are an essential part of academic life. We use them to share our research at conferences, workshops, and faculty seminars. They help us teach effectively in classrooms, deliver public lectures, and communicate our findings to both academic and non-academic audiences. Whether

© The Author(s), under exclusive license to Springer Nature
Switzerland AG 2025
E. Haber et al., *Using AI in Academic Writing and Research*,
https://doi.org/10.1007/978-3-031-91705-9_6

presenting a research paper, leading a discussion, or summarizing key arguments in a grant proposal, presentations serve as a crucial medium for structuring and conveying ideas. A well-crafted presentation can make a significant difference—not only in how our research is received but also in how effectively we engage students, colleagues, and the broader academic community. Clarity, organization, and visual appeal all contribute to making a presentation persuasive and impactful, and make addressing the audience effective (Kaur & Ali, 2017).

Despite their importance, creating high-quality presentations is often a time-consuming and labor-intensive process. Academics frequently spend hours refining slides, structuring content, and ensuring visual coherence (Kmalvand, 2015). Before the advent of generative AI, the process required substantial effort in drafting slides, selecting appropriate visuals, and organizing key points in a way that enhanced understanding. Striking the right balance between text and imagery, maintaining coherence across multiple slides, and ensuring that the presentation aligns with the audience's expectations were all challenges that required careful planning. Even for experienced scholars, the process could be frustrating—especially when preparing multiple presentations for different contexts, such as adapting a research talk for a general audience or restructuring a lecture for a new course.

Generative AI has significantly streamlined this process, making it easier to create well-structured, visually appealing presentations with minimal effort, both for teaching and research purposes (Liu et al., 2024). AI-powered tools can generate slide outlines, suggest relevant content, design layouts, and even refine phrasing for clarity and conciseness (One example is Beautiful.ai, a platform that simplifies the design process by using AI to predict and execute design steps, enhancing data clarity and presentability. It offers pre-built layouts and themes for creating professional-looking presentations quickly). With the right prompts, these tools can assist in adapting a single presentation for different audiences, ensuring that the content remains relevant and engaging. While AI cannot replace thoughtful planning and expert judgment, it can serve as a valuable assistant in optimizing presentation workflows (Barros et al., 2023).

This chapter explores how generative AI can support the creation of academic presentations. We will examine how AI can help with brainstorming, structuring content, designing slides, and refining delivery (Camp & Johnson, 2024). Additionally, we will consider the limitations of AI-generated presentations and discuss strategies for ensuring that AI remains a tool for enhancement rather than a substitute for careful academic communication.

CREATING EFFECTIVE PRESENTATIONS

Generative AI has transformed the process of developing academic presentations by automating content structuring and tailoring materials for different audiences. However, the key to leveraging AI effectively lies in crafting precise prompts that guide it toward generating well-organized, academically sound outlines while preserving the presenter's unique voice and expertise. AI should serve as an assistant, not a substitute, ensuring that presentations remain coherent, engaging, and intellectually rigorous.

For academic audiences, AI can help structure complex research narratives by organizing key findings, methodological approaches, and theoretical frameworks in a logical sequence. When prompted effectively, it can suggest smooth transitions between topics, highlight areas that require further elaboration, and even flag concepts that might need supporting evidence. An example of such a tool is Paperpal—an AI writing assistant designed for academic researchers. It helps in organizing research content, refining language for clarity and conciseness, and ensuring adherence to journal guidelines. This streamlines the process of structuring a compelling argument while ensuring that the depth of analysis remains intact.

Public presentations, by contrast, demand a different approach. Here, the challenge is to translate specialized academic knowledge into an accessible, engaging narrative without sacrificing accuracy. AI can assist by suggesting analogies, simplifying jargon, and identifying explanatory frameworks that make complex ideas more digestible for a general audience. This adaptability allows scholars to tailor their research for broader engagement, whether in public lectures, policy discussions, or interdisciplinary settings. For instance, QuillBot is an AI-driven paraphrasing tool that helps users rephrase sentences, making them clearer and more concise. It's beneficial for simplifying complex academic theories or concepts for a general audience.

A practical example illustrates this workflow: Suppose a researcher is preparing a conference presentation on neural networks. Instead of starting from scratch, they input their research paper into an AI tool, requesting an initial presentation outline. The AI generates a structured framework, identifying key points and proposing relevant visuals. The researcher then refines this outline, using AI to generate simplified explanations for technical concepts and develop audience-appropriate examples. The final product remains their own, but AI has accelerated the process of structuring and refining content.

The effectiveness of AI in presentation development depends on well-crafted prompting strategies. Providing specific instructions—such as details about the audience's expertise, the technical depth required, and the presentation's time constraints—yields more relevant and tailored outputs. However, AI-generated suggestions should never be accepted uncritically. Human oversight is essential to verify accuracy, refine the narrative, and ensure the final presentation aligns with the presenter's scholarly perspective.

Ultimately, success in AI-assisted presentation development requires a balance between automation and human judgment. While AI can generate structural templates and suggest content, the presenter must actively shape and refine these elements to create a coherent, engaging, and academically rigorous presentation. By using AI as a tool to enhance, rather than replace, intellectual effort, scholars can create more effective and impactful presentations with greater efficiency.

Practical Example: Literature Review Presentation Process

Preparing a literature review presentation can be a complex task, requiring the synthesis of multiple sources while maintaining clarity and coherence. Generative AI can assist in streamlining this process by organizing key insights and structuring a compelling narrative. A structured workflow might look like this:

Feed Key Papers into AI – The presenter uploads or summarizes relevant academic papers into an AI tool, prompting it to extract central arguments, theoretical contributions, and methodological insights.

Extract Main Themes and Findings – The AI identifies recurring themes, gaps in the literature, and points of scholarly debate, helping the presenter organize the research landscape.

Generate a Visual Representation of Connections – AI tools such as concept-mapping software or automated slide generators can illustrate how different studies interconnect, highlighting trends, contradictions, and research gaps.

Create a Presentation Narrative – With AI-generated insights as a foundation, the presenter refines the structure, ensuring a logical flow and incorporating their own critical perspective. The AI may assist in drafting slide content, generating explanatory text, or suggesting transitions between topics.

Practical Example: A Researcher Preparing a Presentation on Machine Learning in Healthcare

A researcher preparing a presentation on **machine learning in healthcare** can leverage generative AI to streamline the process and ensure a structured, engaging delivery.

AI analyzes 50 papers to identify recurring themes, such as diagnostic applications, predictive modeling, and challenges in data bias.

Generates visualizations showing research clusters, mapping connections between methodologies, clinical applications, and key innovations.

Creates slides that highlight methodology patterns across studies, illustrating common machine learning techniques and their respective performance metrics.

Suggests gaps in current research, identifying underexplored areas such as the lack of diverse training datasets or challenges in real-world implementation.

Proposes future research directions, outlining emerging trends, such as explainable AI for clinical decision support or federated learning for privacy-preserving healthcare analytics.

Key Outcome: By integrating AI into the preparation process, the researcher transforms an extensive, complex literature review into a **clear, engaging 20-minute presentation**, ensuring that the content remains well-organized, visually compelling, and aligned with academic rigor.

Practical Example: Research Methods Explanation Process

Effectively explaining research methodologies—especially complex or technical ones—requires balancing precision with accessibility. Generative AI can assist in simplifying complex procedures while enhancing clarity through structured visuals and interactive elements. The process can follow these steps:

Input Detailed Methodology – The presenter provides AI with a detailed description of the research methods, including data collection procedures, statistical analyses, and any relevant computational models.

(continued)

(continued)

AI Simplifies Technical Language – AI rephrases dense, jargon-heavy explanations into clearer, more digestible terms without sacrificing accuracy.

Generate Step-by-Step Visual Explanations – AI creates flowcharts, diagrams, or structured slides that illustrate each stage of the methodology, making complex procedures easier to follow.

Create Interactive Elements – AI suggests ways to engage the audience, such as quizzes, real-world applications, or guided discussions, ensuring that methodological concepts resonate with different levels of expertise.

Practical Example: Explaining Complex Statistical Analysis
A researcher preparing to present a **complex statistical analysis** can use AI to enhance clarity and engagement:

AI converts technical procedures into clear language, translating concepts like multiple regression or Bayesian inference into understandable terms.

Creates flowcharts showing decision points, illustrating when to use specific statistical tests based on dataset characteristics.

Generates analogies for complex concepts, such as comparing p-values to a "signal-to-noise" ratio in an experiment.

Suggests audience engagement points, recommending interactive polls or real-world examples to make abstract concepts more tangible.

Develops Q&A anticipation, predicting potential questions from different audience levels and suggesting concise, informative responses.

Key Outcome: By integrating AI into the preparation process, technical research methods can be **presented clearly and effectively to a mixed-expertise audience**, ensuring that both specialists and non-specialists can engage with and understand the material.

Practical Example: Presenting Climate Research
A climate scientist preparing to present findings on **rising sea levels** can use AI to generate audience-specific versions:

Technical version for peer review, including raw data, complex models, and in-depth statistical justifications.

A simplified version for stakeholders, such as environmental organizations, focusing on practical applications and mitigation strategies.

Public version for a general audience, removing jargon and emphasizing key trends and real-world consequences.

Media-friendly version with key takeaways, featuring digestible headlines, concise bullet points, and compelling visuals for news coverage.

Policy brief version focusing on implications, summarizing findings with actionable recommendations for government agencies and policymakers.

Key Outcome: By leveraging AI to tailor research presentations, a **single research project can be effectively communicated to diverse audiences**, maximizing impact and ensuring that findings are accessible, actionable, and relevant to different stakeholders.

While AI plays a crucial role in organizing and refining academic presentations, ensuring that these presentations truly captivate and engage audiences requires more than just clear structure and content. It's about creating an experience that resonates with listeners, leaving a lasting impact. AI can assist in enhancing this "Wow" factor by helping presenters craft compelling narratives, design visually appealing slides, and optimize delivery for maximum engagement. In the next section, we will explore how AI can elevate presentations beyond technical precision, focusing on the stylistic elements that transform a good presentation into a memorable one.

The WOW Effect: Engaging Audiences with AI-Generated Visuals

The **Wow Effect** in presentations goes beyond merely adding AI-generated visuals. It is about capturing attention, evoking curiosity, and making complex ideas instantly clear. AI can enhance this by generating striking, unique visuals tailored to the specific theme of a presentation, avoiding generic stock images. It can create dynamic, high-quality animations that illustrate abstract processes, such as data flows, network models, or environmental simulations. One example of such a tool could be Napkin.ai—a platform that transforms text into insightful visuals instantly, enhancing communication effectiveness. Users can input their text, and Napkin generates relevant visuals such as infographics, diagrams, and flowcharts. AI-generated content can also enhance audience immersion with interactive elements like real-time text-to-image synthesis, live AI-assisted Q&A summaries, or automated visual storytelling. By personalizing presentations, AI enables slides to be adapted to different audiences, simplifying technical data for non-experts while preserving depth for academic discussions. AI-powered tools also contribute to seamless design cohesion, suggesting complementary color schemes, layouts, and typography that enhance readability and visual appeal. A very interesting tool of this type is Khroma, which utilizes AI to learn individual color preferences and generates limitless personalized color palettes. By selecting a set of preferred colors, users train a neural network algorithm that produces harmonious combinations, aiding in consistent and aesthetically pleasing designs.

Beyond standalone AI image-generation platforms, many mainstream commercial tools now incorporate AI-powered features directly into their design workflows. Prezi, PowerPoint, and Canva have integrated AI-assisted functions that help create slides, suggest layouts, generate visual summaries, and even automate animations. These tools make it easier to craft polished, engaging presentations without requiring extensive design expertise. AI in Prezi, for instance, can structure content dynamically, generating visually engaging, non-linear storytelling formats that enhance audience engagement. PowerPoint's AI features assist in organizing slides, recommending visually coherent themes, and even offering automated speech suggestions to refine delivery. Canva streamlines visual refinement by incorporating AI-powered formatting, image enhancement, and automated alignment tools that ensure professional-quality design with minimal effort.

A researcher preparing a presentation on climate change impacts, for example, can leverage AI to maximize engagement. Using Stable Diffusion, they can generate visual scenarios depicting different environmental futures under various policy choices. DALL-E can create conceptual illustrations of carbon capture technologies and mitigation strategies, while AI-powered features in Prezi or PowerPoint can suggest dynamic transitions to navigate between complex datasets and narrative points smoothly. Canva can be used to refine AI-generated visuals into professionally formatted slides, ensuring cohesion and clarity. Motion graphics tools powered by AI can further enhance key takeaways with subtle animations, making data points stand out and reinforcing audience retention.

While AI-generated visuals can significantly enhance engagement, accuracy remains paramount, particularly in academic settings. Effective prompting techniques are essential to ensure that AI-generated images align with scientific standards, historical accuracy, and theoretical validity. Cross-referencing AI-generated visuals with established academic sources helps maintain credibility, ensuring that AI serves as a tool to enhance comprehension rather than merely adding aesthetic appeal. The most effective academic presentations use AI-generated content purposefully, integrating it to strengthen arguments, clarify complex ideas, and create a lasting impression on the audience.

Examples illustrate how AI-generated visuals can transform academic presentations, making complex topics more accessible and engaging. One application is molecular structure animation, where AI converts static molecular data into dynamic 3D visualizations. In a protein folding presentation, AI can generate accurate 3D protein models, create step-by-step folding animations, and add interactive elements highlighting binding sites. The MOE has these capabilities—it is a comprehensive software system that integrates visualization, modeling, and simulations for molecular structures. It offers tools for protein modeling, allowing users to create step-by-step folding animations and interactive elements highlighting binding sites. Multiple viewing angles provide a deeper understanding of structural changes. The process involves using Stable Diffusion for initial renders, refining them with specialized molecular visualization tools, and adding motion effects. The result is a presentation where complex molecular interactions become instantly comprehensible.

Another example is historical data reconstruction, which transforms archival data into visual narratives. In an archaeological site reconstruction,

AI can generate accurate period-specific visualizations, create before-and-after site comparisons, and show evolutionary changes over time. Human scale references and environmental context enhance realism. For instance, CyArk can help scientists with this—it is a non-profit organization that leverages advanced technologies, including AI, to create detailed 3D models of cultural heritage sites worldwide, aiding in preservation and visualization of historical landmarks. This process typically involves using DALL-E for initial concept images, refining them through architectural accuracy checks, and structuring a timeline progression. The outcome is a compelling historical reconstruction that transforms static data into an engaging visual story.

A final example is climate change impact visualization, where predictive models are converted into visual scenarios. For an urban climate impact presentation, AI-generated city-specific visuals can illustrate progressive environmental changes over decades. A great example of such a tool is Destination Earth—an initiative by the European Commission, DestinE aims to create a digital simulation of Earth with a digital twin that will be used to better understand the effects of climate change and environmental disasters. Split-screen comparisons highlight key transformations, while data overlays provide essential metrics such as temperature shifts and rising sea levels. Human impact indicators further contextualize the data. This approach combines Midjourney for base images with additional data visualization layers to ensure scientific accuracy. By making abstract climate projections tangible and relatable, these presentations help diverse audiences grasp the real-world implications of environmental change.

AI AND SOCIAL MEDIA

AI has become an essential tool for academics seeking to enhance their social media presence, offering efficient ways to amplify research visibility while maintaining scholarly integrity. As social media increasingly shapes academic discourse, AI assists in translating complex findings into engaging, accessible content suited to different platforms with minimal effort. By strategically integrating AI tools, researchers can maximize impact without requiring extensive time or specialized communication skills. One example can be NotebookLM, an AI-powered note-taking tool developed by Google Labs, designed to help users understand complex information by summarizing multiple sources, suggesting follow-up questions, and creating study guides, thereby aiding in the effective communication of research findings.

One of the most effective approaches is uploading an article or research summary into a generative AI tool and prompting it to adapt the content for different media platforms and audiences. For Twitter/X, AI can distill key findings into concise, high-impact threads with compelling hooks. For LinkedIn, it can develop professional, thought-provoking posts that engage both academic and industry audiences. For visually driven platforms such as Instagram or YouTube, AI can generate research summaries in infographic format, create short explainer videos, or adapt findings into engaging slides. For instance, NoteGPT is an AI summarizer and generator that enhances learning by quickly summarizing content from various sources, including YouTube videos, PDFs, articles, and PowerPoint presentations. AI-powered writing tools can also suggest captions, refine tone, and ensure clarity while preserving the researcher's expertise.

AI extends beyond text by enabling the creation of custom visuals tailored to a specific study. Platforms like DALL-E and MidJourney allow researchers to generate unique images that visually represent key concepts, making academic work more shareable and appealing. A researcher studying climate change, for example, could create AI-generated depictions of rising temperatures in urban settings or visual comparisons of different environmental futures. Similarly, those working on historical topics could use AI to generate reconstructions of ancient sites or theoretical models. By pairing AI-generated visuals with AI-optimized text, researchers can present their work in a more compelling and accessible way.

AI-driven content optimization also enhances reach and engagement. AI tools analyze audience behavior to determine the best posting times, recommend hashtags, and refine messaging based on engagement trends. Automated response suggestions help maintain consistent interaction with followers, ensuring that research discussions remain active and dynamic. There is a very interesting tool for this—Brand24 is a social listening and media monitoring tool that tracks hashtag performance in real time across various platforms. It provides insights into hashtag popularity, reach, and sentiment, aiding in refining your hashtag strategy.

The potential for AI in research communication is virtually limitless. Academics can experiment with generative AI to create interactive polls based on their studies, generate Q&A formats that simplify complex arguments, or even develop AI-assisted blog posts summarizing key insights. With AI-assisted workflows, research dissemination no longer has to be a time-consuming process—AI helps bridge the gap between rigorous scholarship and broad accessibility. One example can be Writesonic, an AI writing tool that assists in creating various content forms, including articles, blogs, and social media posts. Researchers can utilize Writesonic to develop AI-assisted blog posts that summarize key insights from their studies, enhancing the dissemination of complex information.

Despite these advantages, human oversight remains essential. While AI can generate content efficiently, scholars must ensure that messaging remains accurate and aligned with their research. The goal is not to let AI replace academic voices but to enhance them, making research more approachable without compromising intellectual depth. By embracing AI as a tool for accessibility and engagement, scholars can transform their research into widely shared and influential content while maintaining scholarly rigor.

PRESENTATION DESIGN AND STRUCTURE

Creating effective presentations with AI requires more than simply generating slides with compelling visuals and structured text. While AI tools offer powerful design capabilities, maintaining clarity, accessibility, and coherence is essential to ensuring that presentations serve their academic purpose rather than becoming visually overwhelming. A well-designed presentation enhances understanding, supports key arguments, and keeps the audience engaged without distraction.

Ensuring visual accessibility is a fundamental step in presentation design. Readability and contrast should always be optimized, taking into account the conditions in which the presentation will be viewed. High-contrast text improves legibility, especially in projected settings where lighting conditions can be unpredictable. Color selection should be tested using accessibility verification tools to ensure that slides remain clear for all viewers, including those with visual impairments. Typography should also be scaled appropriately based on the audience's viewing distance to prevent strain and maintain engagement.

Data visualization must go beyond merely inserting charts into slides. Choosing the right visual representation for data is crucial, as poorly selected charts can misrepresent findings or make interpretation difficult. AI-powered tools assist in selecting the most appropriate chart types based on data characteristics, transforming numerical results into intuitive visual narratives. However, thoughtful design remains necessary to ensure that charts are meaningful rather than decorative.

Maintaining design coherence is equally important. While AI enables a high degree of creativity, excessive variation in fonts, colors, and graphical elements can make slides appear disjointed and reduce their effectiveness. Rather than incorporating multiple design styles, presenters should establish a unified visual language by applying consistent colors, geometric elements, and image treatments throughout. This approach not only creates a polished aesthetic but also ensures that visual cues reinforce the content rather than distract from it.

Color strategy is another consideration in presentation design. A focused color palette, typically consisting of two or three primary hues, enhances both aesthetic appeal and readability. Following established design principles, presenters can allocate approximately 60 percent of the color scheme to a dominant shade, 30 percent to a secondary color, and 10 percent to accents that highlight key points. This structured approach mirrors the way professional designers balance visual composition, ensuring that slides remain engaging while preserving clarity. For instance, Huemint utilizes machine learning to create unique color schemes tailored for branding, websites, or graphics. Users can generate palettes that align with specific design principles, ensuring a balanced and visually appealing presentation.

Typography should be handled with similar restraint. Selecting one or two complementary typefaces ensures readability and prevents slides from appearing inconsistent. When multiple fonts are used, they should contrast in a meaningful way, such as pairing a bold display font for headings with a clean, legible typeface for body text. Typeface personality should align with the presentation's subject matter—formal presentations benefit from classic, professional fonts, while more creative topics allow for expressive type choices. For example, Monotype can help with this—it is an AI-driven tool that assists designers in finding harmonious typeface combinations. It considers typographic attributes like stroke contrast and proportions to recommend pairs that align with the presentation's subject matter, ensuring that typeface personalities match the intended tone.

An effective slide functions as a visual aid rather than a full-text document. Presenters should avoid overwhelming viewers with excessive textual content, treating each slide as a guidepost rather than a full explanation. If a topic requires detailed elaboration, breaking content into multiple slides is preferable to condensing it into dense lists. Negative space should be embraced to maintain clarity, drawing attention to key points rather than cluttering the layout with excessive information.

Visual communication should be approached strategically. Images, icons, and graphics should reinforce the presentation's core messages rather than serve as mere decoration. Research suggests that visual processing occurs significantly faster than textual comprehension, meaning that well-placed images can enhance understanding and retention. AI-generated visuals, such as illustrations created with DALL-E or Stable Diffusion, can be particularly effective in academic contexts where standard stock images may not capture the nuances of a specific topic.

A more original approach to presentation design often yields stronger engagement. Instead of relying on conventional stock images or overused visual metaphors, AI can be used to generate unique illustrations that align with research topics. Even within structured institutional branding guidelines, creative expression is possible through the thoughtful selection of imagery, layout, and animations. One example can be SlideSpeak's AI, is a presentation maker, which includes a custom branding feature that allows users to incorporate specific colors, fonts, and logos into their presentations. This ensures adherence to institutional branding guidelines while enabling the creation of visually appealing and unique presentations. AI-powered platforms such as Prezi, Canva, and PowerPoint provide a range of intelligent design suggestions, allowing presenters to achieve a professional aesthetic without requiring advanced design skills.

Structuring a presentation effectively requires logical progression and clear sectioning. Distinct opening and closing segments help frame the content, while smooth transitions between topics maintain coherence. AI tools can assist in structuring presentations by suggesting optimal sequencing of information, identifying potential gaps, and recommending transition slides that improve flow. For example, Gamma provides AI-driven assistance in creating presentations, offering guided, step-by-step workflows. It helps users structure their content effectively, ensuring a logical flow and coherence between slides.

Selecting the right AI tools depends on the complexity of the content and the desired presentation format. Researchers working with intricate visuals, such as structural diagrams or predictive models, may benefit from high-resolution image-generation tools like Midjourney or DALL-E. For presentations requiring rapid iteration, user-friendly platforms like Canva provide efficient templates and drag-and-drop functionality that streamline the design process. AI-powered animation tools can also enhance engagement by creating subtle motion effects that reinforce key messages.

By strategically leveraging AI, academics can enhance not only presentations but also their broader research communication efforts. Uploading research papers to generative AI platforms enables adaptation to different media formats, making complex findings more accessible to wider audiences. AI can transform long-form research into social media-friendly posts, generate visuals for online engagement, and suggest platform-specific adaptations tailored for academic and public audiences. One interesting example is Narrato: it offers a comprehensive suite of AI content creation and management tools, enabling users to transform existing content into various formats suitable for different channels. This includes repurposing research papers into blog posts, social media updates, or summaries, facilitating wider dissemination of research findings.

A structured approach to AI-assisted social media strategy allows researchers to maximize visibility while maintaining academic credibility. Defining clear objectives and identifying target audiences ensures that content aligns with research dissemination goals, whether the aim is to promote a recent publication, foster interdisciplinary collaboration, or engage the public in critical discussions. AI-generated content drafts help streamline the writing process, while platforms like ChatGPT or Gemini assist in adjusting tone and style based on the chosen medium. AI tools further enhance engagement by optimizing visuals, suggesting hashtags, and analyzing performance metrics to refine content strategy. For instance, Flick offers AI-driven content creation, including caption generation and hashtag optimization. It identifies top-performing hashtags for your posts, aiding in maximizing reach and engagement.

For example, a researcher launching a paper on AI ethics could use AI to generate a Twitter thread breaking down key findings into an engaging series of posts. AI-generated visual abstracts could be shared on Instagram, while a more detailed article could be posted on LinkedIn. By scheduling posts at optimal times and using AI-powered analytics to track engagement, researchers can significantly expand the reach of their work while maintaining meaningful academic discourse. In that domain, Buffer offers AI-driven features that tailor posts to each social media channel. It analyzes audience engagement patterns to suggest optimal posting times and recommends relevant hashtags, enhancing content visibility and interaction.

AI also facilitates real-time engagement during conferences, where summarizing key presentations and discussions can be challenging. Generative AI can assist in creating quick summaries of conference talks, producing visual overviews, and generating multilingual adaptations of key takeaways. For instance, Notta AI offers a comprehensive solution for transcribing and summarizing audio content, including conference talks. Scientists can upload recordings, and the platform provides real-time transcriptions alongside concise summaries, facilitating quick insights and efficient information retrieval. Live content generation, such as instant polls or discussion prompts, helps create interactive conference communities that extend beyond in-person attendees.

Research labs and academic institutions can also benefit from AI-driven content strategies to maintain a consistent digital presence. AI can automate the creation of weekly research updates, behind-the-scenes lab insights, and short videos explaining technical concepts. Automated responses help maintain audience engagement, while AI-generated Q&A sessions allow for interactive discussions on complex topics.

Key success metrics for AI-assisted research dissemination extend beyond traditional social media engagement. Increased citations, expanded professional networks, and greater interdisciplinary collaboration are meaningful indicators of AI's role in academic impact. By embracing AI-powered tools for research communication, academics can bridge the gap between specialized scholarship and broader public engagement, ensuring that their work reaches the right audiences with clarity, precision, and lasting influence. Semantic Scholar, developed by the Allen Institute for Artificial Intelligence, is an AI-powered search engine that enhances the discovery of scientific literature. It utilizes natural language processing to provide concise summaries of academic papers, helping researchers and the general public quickly grasp complex topics.

EMERGING TRENDS AND FUTURE DIRECTIONS

The future of scientific visualization is being reshaped by advances in AI, immersive media, and interactive data presentation. These emerging technologies are transforming how researchers communicate complex data, moving beyond static visuals toward dynamic, real-time, and three-dimensional experiences that enhance both comprehension and engagement.

AI-driven 3D visualization tools are at the forefront of this transformation. By converting complex datasets into intuitive, explorable models, these tools allow researchers to present findings in ways that are more interactive and engaging. Machine learning algorithms can analyze vast amounts of data, identifying patterns and relationships that would be difficult to detect manually. These AI-generated visual representations highlight key insights, adapting dynamically as new information becomes available. In fields such as genomics, climate science, and particle physics, where datasets are massive and constantly evolving, AI-driven visualizations provide a level of clarity that traditional methods struggle to achieve.

Virtual and augmented reality further expands the possibilities of scientific communication. Virtual reality environments allow researchers to create immersive experiences where audiences can step inside data visualizations, molecular structures, or theoretical models (Immersive Science develops VR applications tailored for scientific research, including tools for biomedical and astronomical data visualization. Their platforms enable users to interact with complex datasets in an immersive environment, enhancing data interpretation and hypothesis generation). Augmented reality applications, on the other hand, overlay digital information onto physical spaces, making it possible to conduct interactive demonstrations or present real-time data overlays during live talks. These technologies are already finding applications in medical research, where AR is used for surgical planning, and in environmental science, where VR is being employed to create immersive climate change models. Astronomers are developing interactive stellar mapping systems, while molecular biologists are leveraging 3D visualization to study protein interactions with unprecedented detail.

As AI and immersive technologies continue to evolve, the challenge lies in balancing innovation with practicality. While these tools offer new ways to engage with complex data, their effectiveness will ultimately depend on how seamlessly they integrate into research communication. The goal is not to overwhelm audiences with technological complexity but to enhance scientific understanding through more intuitive, accessible, and meaningful visualization techniques.

Looking ahead, emerging technologies such as neural interfaces, quantum-powered visualization, and AI-driven holography promise to push the boundaries of how research is presented and experienced.

Neural interface presentations offer a potential shift in how data is communicated. Current implementations already allow EEG data to drive real-time visualization changes, while thought-controlled navigation through datasets enables a more intuitive interaction with complex information. Neural feedback mechanisms can adjust the pace of a presentation based on audience engagement, dynamically adapting content in response to real-time attention monitoring. Future advancements may enable collaborative neural networking, where multiple users can interact with data simultaneously, leading to shared experiential visualization and real-time audience feedback based on neural signals. While early implementations exist, full integration of neural interfaces into academic presentations is expected within the next seven to ten years.

Quantum computing is set to revolutionize data visualization by enabling the processing of multidimensional datasets in real time. Current capabilities include quantum-based pattern recognition, probabilistic data modeling, and interactive quantum simulations. In the coming years, quantum-enhanced real-time modeling will allow researchers to conduct instantaneous data visualization on previously unmanageable scales. Potential applications include multi-universe data comparison in physics, instantaneous genetic analysis in biology, and advanced climate simulations. While basic quantum-powered visualization tools are expected within the next two to three years, more sophisticated applications will likely take five to seven years to reach widespread adoption.

AI-driven holographic research presentations offer another promising avenue for the future of scientific communication. Current technologies already allow for basic volumetric displays, gesture-controlled interactions, and multi-user viewing capabilities. Remote holographic presence is emerging as a viable alternative to traditional virtual conferencing, enabling speakers to deliver presentations as life-sized, three-dimensional projections. The next stage of development will likely include full-room holographic environments, tactile interaction with holographic models, and AI-driven narrative adaptation that adjusts the presentation based on audience engagement. Within four to six years, these technologies are expected to evolve into sophisticated research communication tools, making it possible for researchers to collaborate across locations in real-time holographic environments.

These emerging trends suggest that the future of scientific visualization will not be defined by a single breakthrough but by the convergence of multiple technologies. As AI, immersive media, and advanced computing capabilities continue to develop, research presentations will become more interactive, adaptive, and accessible, fundamentally changing how knowledge is communicated across disciplines.

Best Practices and Workflow Integration

Effectively integrating AI-generated visualizations into research workflows requires a systematic approach that balances automation, quality control, and project-specific needs. Selecting the right AI tool involves evaluating project complexity, available time, and quality expectations. For highly detailed visualizations that require precision, more sophisticated AI tools may provide superior results but often demand more time and iterative refinement. In contrast, simpler projects may benefit from faster, automated tools that prioritize efficiency over customization.

Time investment varies significantly across AI platforms. Some tools generate quick results using template-based approaches, requiring minimal user input, while others demand detailed prompting, iterative fine-tuning, and expert validation. The selection should align with project deadlines and available resources, factoring in both learning curves for new tools and the time required for quality assurance.

Version control is critical when collaborating on AI-enhanced scientific illustrations. Establishing clear naming conventions and documentation practices ensures that different versions of AI-generated content are systematically tracked. Maintaining a record of prompts, generation parameters, and refinements improves reproducibility and facilitates future adjustments. Storing both raw AI outputs and finalized versions in an organized manner allows for seamless updates and reference when needed.

Collaboration in AI-assisted visualization requires structured workflows. Clearly defining roles within a research team streamlines the process—some members may focus on content generation, while others handle accuracy verification, refinement, and design consistency. Centralized access to visualization resources and shared editing platforms facilitate real-time collaboration. Regular review checkpoints and structured feedback loops enhance both the scientific accuracy and visual clarity of AI-generated content.

Attribution and licensing are essential considerations when using AI-generated materials. It is important to document which elements were AI-generated and which tools were used, ensuring compliance with platform-specific licensing terms. Transparency in attribution when publishing or presenting AI-assisted work reinforces ethical research practices. Maintaining records of usage rights and permissions avoids potential copyright or ethical concerns associated with AI-generated content.

Quality assurance protocols play a fundamental role in ensuring that AI-generated visualizations align with scientific standards. Regular review checkpoints should be integrated throughout the workflow, with subject matter experts verifying both the accuracy of representations and their clarity for intended audiences. While AI-generated visuals should enhance engagement, they must also meet rigorous educational and scientific criteria. Striking a balance between visual appeal and accuracy is crucial for maintaining credibility in research dissemination.

One example of an AI-integrated workflow is a **research data visualization pipeline**. The process begins with uploading raw research data into an AI-powered visualization tool, where it is pre-processed using standardized techniques. The initial AI-generated visualizations undergo verification for scientific accuracy before being refined with design tools to ensure consistency in color schemes, labels, and overall presentation quality. A researcher working in genomics, for instance, may upload sequencing data to an AI tool specializing in network visualizations, refine the output based on expert feedback, and finalize the visuals for inclusion in a publication or conference presentation. Documentation at each stage—including AI prompts, tool settings, and review notes—ensures reproducibility and transparency.

Another key strategy is **multi-platform content adaptation**, where AI is used to tailor research findings for various dissemination channels. This process starts with a core research summary, which is then adapted using AI tools for different formats while maintaining factual accuracy. A researcher might generate a comprehensive LinkedIn article for professional audiences, a concise Twitter thread for quick insights, and an AI-assisted slide deck for conference presentations. Ensuring factual consistency across all versions, applying institutional branding, and coordinating a strategic release schedule enhances research visibility while maintaining integrity. Engagement metrics from each platform provide valuable insights for refining future content strategies.

For collaborative projects, **AI-assisted presentation development** can streamline the visualization process while ensuring accuracy and coherence. Structuring team roles around AI tool expertise and subject knowledge optimizes efficiency. One workflow could involve an AI specialist generating preliminary visualizations, a subject expert verifying scientific accuracy, a design specialist refining visual elements, and a team lead ensuring the final presentation maintains a cohesive narrative. A shared workspace with clear version control practices allows for consistent refinement and adaptation. Creating reusable AI-assisted templates for common visualization types, such as molecular structures, climate models, or statistical comparisons, further enhances long-term efficiency.

Several factors contribute to the success of AI-assisted visualization workflows. Maintaining clear documentation of AI tool settings and prompts ensures reproducibility and standardization. Establishing consistent quality control checkpoints prevents inaccuracies from propagating into final outputs. Effective team communication channels facilitate collaboration across roles, while systematic version control practices allow for iterative refinement. Striking the right balance between automation and human oversight is key to ensuring that AI-generated content enhances research communication rather than replacing critical expertise. Finally, continuous evaluation and optimization of AI-assisted workflows ensure that researchers maximize both efficiency and scientific rigor in their visualization strategies.

CONCLUSION

Generative AI has reshaped the way academics create and deliver presentations, making the process more efficient while opening new possibilities for engagement and communication. By assisting with content structuring, slide design, and audience adaptation, AI allows researchers to focus more on refining their message rather than spending excessive time on formatting and layout. The ability to tailor a single presentation for different audiences, generate clear and compelling visuals, and optimize delivery makes AI an invaluable tool for academic communication.

However, the effectiveness of AI-generated presentations depends on thoughtful implementation. While AI can streamline workflows and enhance visual appeal, it cannot replace human judgment, domain expertise, or the ability to convey complex ideas with nuance. Successful academic presentations still require careful planning, strategic use of AI-generated content, and rigorous quality control to ensure accuracy and scholarly integrity. Maintaining a balance between automation and human oversight is crucial in preventing AI-generated errors from undermining the credibility of research.

Beyond traditional slides, emerging trends in AI visualization, immersive technologies, and dynamic presentation formats signal a shift toward more interactive and adaptive academic communication. As tools continue to evolve, researchers will have even more opportunities to leverage AI for real-time audience engagement, multi-platform content dissemination, and novel approaches to scientific storytelling. The integration of AI into research presentations is not just about efficiency—it is about enhancing clarity, fostering engagement, and ultimately making complex ideas more accessible to diverse audiences.

While AI offers remarkable possibilities, it remains a tool rather than a replacement for scholarly communication. Thoughtful integration, ethical considerations, and ongoing refinement will determine how effectively academics harness AI to improve the impact and reach of their presentations. As AI-driven tools continue to develop, academics who embrace these advancements with a critical and strategic approach will be best positioned to communicate their research with clarity, authority, and lasting influence.

References

Barros, A., Prasad, A., & Śliwa, M. (2023). Generative artificial intelligence and academia: Implication for research, teaching and service. *Management Learning, 54*(5), 597–604.

Camp, J. W., & Johnson, H. (2024). AI as designated designer: Training public-speaking students to use Beautiful.ai for their slide presentations. *Communication Teacher*, (August), 1–5.

Kaur, K., & Ali, A. M. (2017). Exploring the genre of academic oral presentations: A critical review. *International Journal of Applied Linguistics & English Literature, 7*(1), 152.

Kmalvand, A. (2015). Visual communication in powerpoint presentations in applied linguistics. *TechTrends : For Leaders in Education & Training, 59*(6), 41–45.

Liu, Y., Park, J., & McMinn, S. (2024). Using generative artificial intelligence/ChatGPT for academic communication: Students' perspectives. *International Journal of Applied Linguistics, 34*(4), 1437–1461.

CHAPTER 7

Future Trends and Emerging Tools

Abstract This chapter examines the rapidly evolving future of generative AI in academia, mapping key technological trends and emerging tools that are reshaping research, teaching, and scholarly communication. From advances in explainable AI, transfer learning, and quantum computing to the integration of AR/VR and AI-assisted big data analytics, the chapter explores how AI is enabling interdisciplinary collaboration, immersive education, and personalized research workflows. It also addresses the intersection of AI with open science, emphasizing data harmonization, decentralized collaboration, and ethical considerations. While AI promises unprecedented innovation, the chapter cautions that its integration must be critically guided by transparency, accountability, and scholarly rigor to ensure equitable and trustworthy academic practices.

Keywords Future of AI • Academic innovation • Explainable AI • Quantum computing • Interdisciplinary research • Augmented reality • Big data • Open science • Federated learning • Academic ethics

Technology is evolving at an extraordinary pace. Even in the process of writing this book, generative AI has undergone significant advancements, with new models, features, and applications emerging almost daily. Companies continue to announce breakthroughs, release more powerful

© The Author(s), under exclusive license to Springer Nature Switzerland AG 2025
E. Haber et al., *Using AI in Academic Writing and Research*,
https://doi.org/10.1007/978-3-031-91705-9_7

models, and refine AI's capabilities, making it clear that we are only at the beginning of what this technology can achieve. The rapid iteration of AI models means that what was cutting-edge a few months ago may soon become obsolete, replaced by more sophisticated systems with greater accuracy, efficiency, and adaptability.

Admittedly, predicting where this road will lead remains a challenge. While some trends appear inevitable—such as AI becoming more autonomous, multimodal, and seamlessly integrated into academic workflows—the specifics of how these developments will unfold remain uncertain. Will AI systems become fully embedded into research environments, automating entire aspects of academic work? Will AI-generated content become indistinguishable from human output, raising new ethical and regulatory concerns? How will institutions and publishers adapt to these transformations? Will they embrace them, or slide into AI shaming (Giray, 2024)? These questions highlight the unpredictability of AI's trajectory and the need for academics to stay informed and adaptable.

In this chapter, we will explore some of the most promising and transformative trends shaping the future of AI in academia (Budhwani, 2024). From emerging AI models and visualization technologies to collaborative AI agents and advanced research tools, we will map out key developments that scholars should be aware of. While it is impossible to predict every turn in this evolving landscape, understanding these trends will help academics navigate the next wave of technological change, ensuring that they are prepared to integrate AI into their work effectively and responsibly, and use AI to support rather than replace their own work (Thaichana et al., 2025).

TECHNOLOGICAL ADVANCEMENTS

AI is evolving at an extraordinary pace, reshaping academic practices with more intelligent algorithms and automation (Gupta et al., 2024). Advances in natural language processing, machine learning, and deep learning are leading to increasingly sophisticated AI tools that can assist researchers and educators in ways previously unimaginable (Zahra & Rautela, 2024). These tools can automate tedious tasks, analyze vast amounts of data in seconds, and generate insights that would be difficult—or even impossible—for humans to uncover alone (Laxmi et al., 2024). For instance, AI-driven literature review tools can scan thousands of academic papers, identify relevant studies, extract key findings, and even propose new hypotheses (Lytras et al., 2024), significantly accelerating the research process (Robledo et al., 2021). (In that case, it is worth using the Research Rabbit, which is an AI research assistant that assists researchers in discovering and organizing academic papers efficiently, offering interactive visualizations, collaborative exploration, and personalized recommendations to facilitate comprehensive literature reviews.)

Beyond research, AI-powered adaptive learning platforms and intelligent tutoring systems are transforming education by tailoring learning experiences to individual students. These systems analyze student performance, detect knowledge gaps, and dynamically adjust instruction to optimize comprehension and retention. The result is a more personalized and efficient learning environment where students receive targeted support based on their specific needs. As AI continues to develop, we can expect tools that interact with students in even more intuitive ways, understanding complex natural language queries, generating human-like explanations, and adapting dynamically to different learning styles.

One of the most exciting frontiers in AI development is the potential impact of quantum computing. Unlike classical computers, quantum computers process information in fundamentally different ways, enabling them to perform calculations at unprecedented speeds. This could revolutionize AI by accelerating the training of large models, enhancing their ability to solve complex problems, and opening new possibilities in fields such as drug discovery, materials science, and financial modeling. While still in its early stages, quantum AI holds the promise of breakthroughs that could fundamentally alter the landscape of academic research.

As these advancements unfold, it is crucial for academics to stay informed about emerging AI tools and their potential applications. Those who embrace AI can significantly enhance their research and teaching, leveraging automation and intelligent analysis to work more efficiently and uncover new insights. However, the growing reliance on AI also raises critical questions. The need for **explainability, accountability, and ethical considerations** becomes increasingly important as AI takes on more complex roles in academia. Scholars must navigate the balance between AI's benefits and the essential role of human expertise, ensuring that AI enhances rather than diminishes scholarly rigor.

Several emerging AI techniques are particularly relevant to academic research:

Explainable AI (XAI) addresses one of the major challenges in AI adoption—the so-called black box problem. Many machine learning models generate results without offering insight into how they reached their conclusions, making it difficult for researchers to verify their validity. Explainable AI aims to develop models that are more transparent and interpretable, allowing academics to trust and understand AI-generated findings. Techniques such as feature importance analysis and decision tree visualization help reveal which variables most influence AI predictions. Additionally, AI-generated natural language explanations can summarize complex model behavior in more intuitive terms. As these methods improve, AI will become a more reliable and widely accepted tool in academic research.

Transfer learning is another transformative AI capability, enabling models trained on one dataset or task to be quickly adapted for new domains with minimal additional training. This is particularly valuable in research areas where high-quality training data is scarce. By leveraging pre-trained models and fine-tuning them on smaller, domain-specific datasets, researchers can develop AI tools without the need for extensive data collection and annotation. For instance, a model trained on a broad scientific literature database can be refined to identify specific types of experimental results or methodologies, significantly reducing the time researchers spend reviewing and synthesizing prior work. As transfer learning becomes more accessible, it will lower barriers to AI adoption, making advanced AI-driven research tools available to a wider academic community.

AI is no longer a distant technological prospect—it is already embedded in academic workflows, with capabilities that continue to expand. The challenge for scholars is not simply to keep up with these changes but to actively engage with AI in ways that enhance their work while maintaining academic integrity. The next wave of AI innovation will likely bring even more powerful tools, and those who understand how to harness these technologies will be at the forefront of the future of research and education.

INTERDISCIPLINARY OPPORTUNITIES

AI is dissolving the traditional boundaries between academic disciplines, fostering collaboration in ways that were previously unimaginable. By providing powerful tools for data analysis, pattern recognition, and knowledge discovery, AI enables researchers from diverse fields to work together on complex, multifaceted problems that require expertise from multiple domains (KNIME is an open-source platform that integrates various components for machine learning and data mining, allowing researchers to visually create data flows and analyze large datasets without extensive programming knowledge). Whether in the humanities, social sciences, or natural sciences, AI is facilitating new modes of inquiry, helping scholars uncover insights that would have been difficult—or impossible—to achieve through conventional methods alone.

One striking example of AI-driven interdisciplinary research is in the **digital humanities**, where AI is revolutionizing the analysis of historical texts, images, and artifacts (Chun & Elkins, 2023), as well as the emergence of computational social sciences (Gefen et al., 2021; Jemielniak, 2020). Researchers in literature, history, and computer science are using machine learning algorithms to detect patterns in ancient manuscripts, uncover hidden relationships between texts, and reconstruct lost cultural narratives (Transkribus is an AI-powered platform designed for the transcription, recognition, and analysis of historical documents. It enables automated transcription of handwritten texts, facilitating the digitization and study of manuscripts across various languages and periods). AI-assisted handwriting recognition, for instance, has been instrumental in deciphering previously unreadable scripts, opening new avenues for historical and linguistic research. In **computational linguistics**, AI-driven models are allowing scholars in psychology, neuroscience, and language sciences to study the intricacies of human cognition, advancing our understanding of how language shapes thought. Sociology and anthropology is embracing insights into human behavior previously unachievable.

Beyond the humanities and social sciences, AI is driving interdisciplinary breakthroughs in **bioinformatics**, where it is accelerating the analysis of genomic and clinical data. By integrating expertise from biology, medicine, and computer science, researchers are using AI to identify disease markers, develop precision treatments, and generate new insights into genetic disorders. In **environmental science**, AI models are being employed to simulate ecological systems, track climate patterns, and predict the effects of environmental changes with unprecedented accuracy. (An excellent example of such a solution is CoreDiff—an AI-based weather forecasting model that enhances the accuracy of predicting hazardous weather by focusing from national to local scales. This model enables rapid and efficient ultra-high-resolution weather simulations, significantly improving short- to medium-range forecasts.) These collaborations are essential for addressing global challenges, such as climate change and public health crises, where no single discipline holds all the answers.

As AI continues to evolve, new interdisciplinary opportunities will emerge, allowing researchers to work across fields in ways that challenge existing academic silos. However, interdisciplinary work is not without its challenges. Differences in terminology, research methodologies, and epistemological approaches can create barriers to effective collaboration. Ensuring that researchers from different disciplines share a common framework for communication and interpretation will be critical to maximizing the potential of AI-facilitated research (the AI-Enhanced Research Management, Discovery, and Advisory System (ARDIAS) is a web-based application that provides researchers with a suite of discovery and collaboration tools. It leverages AI to recommend potential collaborators and research topics, facilitating interdisciplinary partnerships). Nevertheless, by fostering dialogue, building interdisciplinary networks, and embracing shared methodologies, scholars can leverage AI to push the frontiers of knowledge in new and exciting directions.

One particularly promising field is **computational archaeology**, where AI is transforming how researchers analyze and interpret ancient artifacts. Machine learning models can process large datasets of archaeological materials, detecting patterns that might otherwise be overlooked. Computer vision algorithms, for instance, can classify and sort pottery fragments based on shape, color, and texture, while natural language processing tools extract insights from historical records and maps. AI is also enabling virtual reconstructions of ancient cities, offering new perspectives on historical urban development and cross-cultural interactions. As these technologies advance, they could allow archaeologists to create predictive models of how past societies responded to environmental and social challenges, offering valuable lessons for the present.

Another groundbreaking application is **AI-assisted drug discovery**, where AI is accelerating the process of identifying and developing new pharmaceuticals. By bringing together experts in chemistry, biology, and computational science, AI-powered drug discovery platforms analyze vast molecular datasets to predict the effectiveness and safety of new drug candidates (Insilico Medicine offers an end-to-end AI-driven drug discovery platform focusing on diseases such as cancer and age-related conditions). Machine learning models trained on libraries of molecular structures and bioactivity data can identify compounds with desirable properties, such as those that bind effectively to disease-related proteins. AI also plays a role in optimizing drug formulations and predicting potential side effects or interactions, significantly reducing the time and cost associated with traditional drug development. By automating many of the most labor-intensive steps in this process, AI is helping to bring life-saving treatments to patients more rapidly and efficiently (Saama Technologies provides AI-driven analytics to enhance various aspects of clinical trials, from patient recruitment to regulatory compliance, improving overall efficiency).

The increasing intersection of AI with multiple academic disciplines signals a shift toward more integrative and collaborative research approaches. By embracing AI as a bridge between fields, scholars can work together in innovative ways, uncovering insights that would not be possible within traditional disciplinary boundaries. As AI tools become more sophisticated, the potential for interdisciplinary breakthroughs will only expand, reshaping not only how research is conducted but also how knowledge itself is structured and understood (Elicit uses AI to help researchers find relevant papers across disciplines and summarize findings. It can analyze research from various fields and highlight connections that might otherwise be missed).

Augmented and Virtual Reality

AI-powered augmented and virtual reality (AR/VR) technologies are revolutionizing education by making learning more immersive, interactive, and experiential. These technologies allow students to engage with complex concepts in ways that traditional methods cannot match—by overlaying digital information onto the real world (AR) or by creating fully simulated environments (VR), they offer dynamic, hands-on learning experiences that deepen understanding and retention (zSpace combines AR/VR with AI to create interactive learning experiences for STEM education, allowing students to manipulate virtual objects that appear to exist in their real environment).

In subjects like history, AR can bring the past to life by allowing students to view 3D models of ancient artifacts and historical sites overlaid onto their physical surroundings. Rather than merely reading about the Parthenon, students can examine a detailed digital reconstruction projected into their classroom, moving around it to explore different architectural elements. In science education, VR enables students to conduct virtual experiments and simulations, manipulating molecules in chemistry or experiencing planetary motion firsthand in astronomy (MEL Chemistry VR allows students to manipulate and explore molecular structures in virtual reality, making abstract chemical concepts tangible and interactive).

These immersive environments remove traditional barriers to learning, allowing students to engage with abstract or inaccessible phenomena in intuitive and exploratory ways.

AI plays a central role in enhancing AR/VR experiences by making them more intelligent and responsive. AI algorithms analyze student interactions in real time, adjusting content difficulty, providing personalized feedback, and guiding students through customized learning pathways. In VR medical training, for example, AI-powered simulations can assess a student's surgical technique, offering corrections and dynamically adjusting difficulty based on performance. AI also enables more realistic and interactive virtual characters and environments, allowing students to engage with responsive historical figures in history lessons or lifelike patient simulations in medical training.

As AR/VR technologies continue to evolve, their applications in education and professional training will expand. Virtual field trips will allow students to visit distant locations without leaving the classroom, while collaborative VR workspaces will enable teams to solve problems together from different locations. AI-driven AR/VR will also improve professional development, offering immersive job training programs tailored to individual learning needs. These tools are poised to redefine how we teach and learn, blending physical and digital experiences to create more engaging and effective educational environments.

Despite these benefits, integrating AR/VR into education presents challenges. Specialized hardware, such as VR headsets and AR-compatible devices, can be costly, limiting accessibility. Cognitive overload and distraction are also concerns, as poorly designed virtual experiences can overwhelm rather than enhance learning. Additionally, it is essential to balance immersive digital experiences with real-world interaction and collaboration, ensuring that students do not become overly reliant on virtual simulations at the expense of hands-on problem-solving. Thoughtful curriculum integration is necessary to maximize the benefits of AR/VR while mitigating potential downsides.

One field already transformed by AI-powered VR is **medical training and simulation**. Virtual reality enables medical students to practice surgical procedures, diagnose virtual patients, and simulate emergency response scenarios in a risk-free, controlled environment. AI enhances these simulations by providing real-time feedback, adjusting complexity based on student performance, and generating realistic patient responses (Osso VR provides realistic surgical training with haptic feedback and AI-driven performance metrics, allowing students to practice procedures and receive objective assessments of their technical skills). A future surgeon can practice an intricate procedure multiple times in VR before ever operating on a real patient, reducing errors and improving patient outcomes. As technology advances, these simulations will become even more sophisticated, integrating haptic feedback for a realistic sense of touch, natural language processing for AI-driven patient interactions, and adaptive learning models that personalize training experiences.

AI-powered AR is also transforming **collaborative design and engineering**, enabling professionals to work together on complex projects without relying solely on physical prototypes. Automotive engineers can use AR to visualize and refine virtual prototypes of new vehicle models, adjusting designs in real time while collaborating across locations (PTC Vuforia Engine provides industrial AR capabilities for automotive prototyping, allowing engineers to visualize full-scale vehicle models in physical space with AI-assisted design optimization). Architects can walk through digital building models projected onto real-world environments, testing different layouts and materials interactively. AI further enhances these experiences through generative design algorithms, which analyze performance criteria and suggest alternative design solutions optimized for cost, efficiency, and sustainability. These AI-driven tools accelerate the design process, reduce material waste, and enable remote collaboration, ultimately driving more innovative and sustainable engineering practices.

As AR/VR and AI continue to advance, their integration will reshape education, research, and professional training. These technologies will not replace traditional learning and design methods but will instead complement them, offering new ways to visualize, interact with, and understand information. By thoughtfully integrating AR/VR into curricula and workflows, educators, researchers, and professionals can harness the power of AI-driven immersive technology to push the boundaries of knowledge, creativity, and innovation.

BIG DATA IN ACADEMIA

AI is fundamentally reshaping the way academics handle and analyze vast datasets, making large-scale research more efficient, accessible, and insightful. The explosion of digital data—from social media posts and financial transactions to satellite imagery and genomic sequences—has created unprecedented opportunities for research but also overwhelming challenges in processing and interpretation. AI-driven big data analytics is transforming this landscape by automating pattern recognition, enhancing predictive modeling, and making sense of complex and unstructured data sources, allowing researchers to uncover insights at a scale and speed that would be impossible through traditional methods.

One of the most powerful applications of AI in big data research is in **data mining and pattern recognition**. AI algorithms can rapidly sift through enormous datasets, identifying trends, correlations, and anomalies that might go unnoticed in manual analysis (RapidMiner—a comprehensive data science platform with AI-powered data mining capabilities that can identify patterns across massive datasets). In social sciences, for instance, natural language processing (NLP) models can analyze millions of social media posts, online discussions, or news articles to track public opinion shifts (Fariello & Jemielniak, 2025), detect emerging societal trends, analyze discourse surrounding political events, or even emerging disasters (Sufi & Khalil, 2024). Similarly, in medical research, AI is helping to detect patterns in patient data that could lead to breakthroughs in diagnostics and personalized treatment (Rajpurkar et al., 2022). AI can analyze thousands of clinical records to uncover early predictors of diseases, optimize treatment strategies, and even suggest previously overlooked connections between genetic markers and health outcomes (Deep Genomics uses AI to decode the meaning of the genome and identify patterns related to disease-causing genetic variants).

Beyond recognizing patterns in existing data, AI is also revolutionizing **predictive modeling and forecasting**. Machine learning models trained on historical data can anticipate future trends with remarkable accuracy, providing valuable insights in disciplines ranging from economics to environmental science. Economists use AI to predict market movements, assess the impact of policy changes, and model macroeconomic risks (Elshendy et al., 2018; Kakkar et al., 2024) (Predata uses AI to analyze digital behavior patterns to predict economic and market movements before they occur). Environmental researchers rely on AI to forecast climate change effects, predict natural disasters, and simulate how ecosystems will respond to different conservation strategies (Materia et al., 2024). These models enable data-driven decision-making that can have far-reaching implications for global policy, business strategy, and public health interventions.

AI's capabilities extend beyond structured numerical datasets to include **unstructured data sources**, such as images, videos, and audio recordings, opening up new research possibilities. Computer vision algorithms are transforming fields like archaeology and art history by analyzing visual patterns across thousands of paintings, manuscripts, or ancient artifacts, identifying stylistic influences and detecting forgeries (Artrendex developed the ArtPI platform that uses AI to identify visual similarities across art collections and detect potential forgeries). In linguistics, AI-driven speech recognition tools are being used to study the evolution of dialects, transcribe endangered languages, and analyze shifts in linguistic patterns over time (Mohanty et al., 2024). In healthcare, AI is revolutionizing radiology by analyzing medical images to detect tumors, fractures, or degenerative conditions with accuracy that rivals human specialists (Mohammed et al., 2024; Prevedello et al., 2019), although the best results are achieved through synergy rather than replacing humans with machines (GLEAMER offers BoneView AI that helps detect fractures and traumatic injuries in X-rays, CT scans, and MRIs).

As the volume and complexity of data continue to grow, AI will become an even more indispensable tool in academic research. By automating labor-intensive aspects of data analysis, AI allows researchers to focus on higher-level theoretical questions, hypothesis generation, and interdisciplinary collaboration. However, the increasing reliance on AI also necessitates critical awareness of its limitations. AI models can inherit biases from the data they are trained on, potentially reinforcing societal inequalities or producing misleading conclusions (Buolamwini, 2024; Gorska & Jemielniak, 2023). Ethical considerations surrounding data privacy, algorithmic transparency, and responsible AI deployment must remain at the forefront of academic discourse. Researchers must not only adopt AI tools but also develop strategies to critically evaluate and validate AI-generated insights, ensuring that data-driven research remains rigorous, fair, and trustworthy.

One example of AI's impact on big data research is **sentiment analysis in social science** (Mahmoudi et al., 2024), where AI-powered NLP models enable scholars to analyze vast amounts of text data to study public sentiment, discourse, and behavioral trends (Lexalytics provides AI-powered text analytics with sentiment analysis capabilities specifically designed for social science research on large datasets). Researchers can train machine learning models to classify millions of social media posts, news articles, or consumer reviews by sentiment—positive, negative, or neutral—uncovering hidden patterns in public opinion. These insights can be used to assess the impact of major political events on public discourse, analyze cultural shifts over time, or even predict consumer behaviors based on sentiment trends in online discussions (Neff & Jemielniak, 2022; Górska et al., 2022) (Pulsar offers AI-powered audience intelligence platform used by political scientists to analyze sentiment across demographic groups and regions). AI-powered sentiment analysis is becoming an essential tool in political science, sociology, and behavioral economics, enabling scholars to work with real-time, large-scale datasets that were previously unmanageable.

AI is also transforming **precision medicine and bioinformatics** (Szulc et al., 2023), allowing researchers to analyze massive amounts of genomic, clinical, and environmental data to develop more personalized and effective treatments. Machine learning models can identify genetic variations linked to specific diseases, predict how different patients will respond to medications, and classify tumors based on molecular profiles for more targeted cancer treatments (Saleh et al., 2020; Lorkowski et al., 2024) (OneOme uses machine learning to analyze genetic data for pharmacogenomic insights, predicting how patients will respond to medications). By integrating diverse datasets—including electronic health records, medical imaging, and wearable device data—AI is creating comprehensive models of human health, enabling early disease detection, predictive diagnostics, and individualized treatment plans. These advances are driving the next generation of data-driven, patient-centered healthcare, improving outcomes while reducing costs and inefficiencies in medical research and clinical practice.

The integration of AI into big data research marks a paradigm shift in how knowledge is generated, interpreted, and applied. As AI models become more sophisticated and datasets continue to expand, academics will need to develop new methodologies for working with these technologies while maintaining a critical perspective on their limitations. AI is not merely a tool for accelerating research—it is reshaping the very nature of academic inquiry, opening new frontiers in data-driven discovery across every field of study.

Open Science and AI

AI is playing an increasingly vital role in advancing the open science movement, which seeks to make research more transparent, accessible, and collaborative. By leveraging AI-powered tools and platforms, researchers can streamline data sharing, improve the discoverability of scientific knowledge, and foster more efficient collaboration across disciplines and institutions. The integration of AI into open science is not only accelerating the pace of discovery but also making scientific research more inclusive and equitable by breaking down barriers to access.

One of the most impactful ways AI is supporting open science is through the development of **open-access repositories and databases**. These platforms rely on AI algorithms to automatically categorize, tag, and organize research outputs, making it easier for scholars to locate relevant studies. AI-driven search and recommendation engines enhance discoverability by identifying connections between studies that might otherwise go unnoticed. (Open Science Framework (OSF): Incorporates AI-powered discovery tools to help researchers find related work across its collaborative platform). Additionally, AI is being used to detect anomalies, inconsistencies, or even potential fraud in research datasets, helping maintain the integrity and reliability of open-access resources.

AI is also **facilitating data sharing and interoperability**, one of the core challenges in open science. Research data is often siloed in different institutions, formatted inconsistently, or structured using domain-specific standards that make integration difficult. AI-powered tools can standardize and harmonize datasets, automatically mapping different formats and terminologies to create more unified and comparable research outputs (Tamr uses machine learning to unify disparate datasets by automatically mapping schemas and standardizing formats across sources). Automated data cleaning and preprocessing tools further reduce the burden on researchers, allowing them to focus on analysis rather than time-consuming data preparation.

Beyond data harmonization, AI is enabling **new forms of collaboration** that were previously impractical. AI-powered platforms can connect researchers across the globe based on their expertise, suggesting potential collaborators for interdisciplinary projects. These systems can analyze publication histories, research interests, and institutional affiliations to match researchers with complementary skills, fostering innovation through cross-disciplinary partnerships. AI is also helping streamline the **peer review process** by intelligently matching submissions with appropriate reviewers, automating aspects of manuscript evaluation, and even detecting potential conflicts of interest (Penelope.ai checks manuscript completeness, reference formatting, and statistical reporting to streamline the peer review process).

As open science continues to gain traction, AI will play an even greater role in fostering transparency, collaboration, and knowledge dissemination. However, these advancements also come with challenges. Ethical concerns surrounding AI's role in determining research visibility, biases in algorithmic decision-making, and issues of data privacy must be carefully addressed. Ensuring that AI-driven open science platforms are governed by clear principles of fairness, accountability, and equity will be essential in making sure the benefits of these technologies are widely and fairly distributed.

One key application of AI in open science is **automated data harmonization,** which addresses one of the biggest challenges in interdisciplinary research—the inconsistency of data formats and standards across different domains and institutions. Machine learning algorithms can help align data elements across diverse schemas and ontologies, while natural language processing tools can extract structured information from unstructured sources, such as research articles or lab notes (LinkSphere employs AI algorithms to identify and align equivalent concepts across different ontologies and data schemas). These AI-driven solutions enable researchers to seamlessly integrate datasets from multiple studies, leading to more comprehensive and reproducible findings. For instance, in biomedical research, AI-powered harmonization techniques allow genetic, clinical, and environmental datasets from different sources to be combined, leading to deeper insights into disease mechanisms and treatment responses (Terra a platform developed by the Broad Institute that uses AI to help researchers harmonize and analyze large-scale genomic and health data).

AI is also driving **decentralized research networks,** which provide alternative models for open and participatory research. Emerging technologies such as blockchain and federated learning are enabling researchers to collaborate on data analysis while maintaining control over their individual datasets. Blockchain-based platforms can facilitate secure and transparent data sharing, ensuring that contributions are properly attributed and reproducible. Federated learning, meanwhile, allows researchers to collaboratively train AI models across multiple institutions without transferring sensitive data to a centralized location (ARTiFACTS: Uses blockchain to establish immutable records of research contributions and data sharing for proper attribution). This decentralized approach to AI-driven research has the potential to make scientific collaboration more secure, inclusive, and scalable, particularly in fields where data privacy and ethical considerations are paramount, such as medical research and social sciences.

By integrating AI into open science practices, researchers can work more effectively, accelerate discovery, and create a more accessible and interconnected scientific community. However, achieving these benefits will require not only technological advancements but also thoughtful governance to ensure that AI-driven tools are used ethically and equitably. With responsible implementation, AI has the potential to democratize science, transforming the way knowledge is shared and expanding the frontiers of human understanding.

CONCLUSION

The integration of AI into academic research is not just a technological shift—it is a fundamental transformation in how knowledge is generated, shared, and applied. From revolutionizing big data analysis to enabling interdisciplinary collaboration, from enhancing open science initiatives to redefining how researchers engage with complex information, AI is reshaping the academic landscape in ways that were once unimaginable.

As AI tools become more sophisticated, they are lowering barriers to entry for researchers, automating time-consuming tasks, and unlocking new possibilities for discovery. The ability to analyze vast datasets, simulate real-world scenarios, and facilitate seamless collaboration across disciplines is accelerating the pace of scientific progress. However, these advancements also raise critical ethical and methodological questions. AI-driven research must be approached with care, ensuring that transparency, accountability, and responsible implementation remain at the core of academic inquiry.

The future of AI in academia will not be defined by any single breakthrough but by the convergence of multiple technologies—big data analytics, explainable AI, quantum computing, and immersive technologies like AR/VR. As these tools continue to evolve, researchers must stay informed, adaptable, and critically engaged with the opportunities and challenges they present. AI is not a replacement for human expertise but an extension of it. The scholars who will thrive in this new era will be those who learn to navigate AI's capabilities while maintaining the rigor, creativity, and ethical responsibility that define academic research.

Ultimately, AI's role in academia is about more than just efficiency—it is about expanding the frontiers of human knowledge. By harnessing AI as a tool for innovation, collaboration, and discovery, researchers can not only push the limits of what is possible but also ensure that science remains open, accessible, and impactful in the years to come.

References

Budhwani, K. I. (2024). The scienthetic method: From Aristotle to AI and the future of medicine. *British Journal of Cancer, 131*(8), 1247–1249.

Buolamwini, J. (2024). *Unmasking AI*. Random House.

Chun, J., & Elkins, K. (2023). The crisis of artificial intelligence: A new digital humanities curriculum for human-centred AI. *International Journal of Humanities and Arts Computing, 17*(2), 147–167.

Elshendy, M., Colladon, A. F., Battistoni, E., & Gloor, P. A. (2018). Using four different online media sources to forecast the crude oil price. *Journal of Information Science and Engineering, 44*(3), 408–421.

Fariello, G., & Jemielniak, D. (2025). The changing language and sentiment of conversations about climate change in reddit posts over sixteen years. *Communications Earth & Environment, 6*(1). https://doi.org/10.1038/s43247-024-01974-8

Gefen, A., Saint-Raymond, L., & Venturini, T. (2021). AI for digital humanities and computational social sciences. In *Reflections on artificial intelligence for humanity* (Lecture notes in computer science) (pp. 191–202). Springer International Publishing.

Giray, L. (2024). AI shaming: The silent stigma among academic writers and researchers. *Annals of Biomedical Engineering, 52*(9), 2319–2324.

Gorska, A. M., & Jemielniak, D. (2023). The invisible women: Uncovering gender bias in AI-generated images of professionals. *Feminist Media Studies, 23*(8), 4370–4375.

Górska, A., Kulicka, K., & Jemielniak, D. (2022). Men NOT going their own way: A thick big data analysis of #MGTOW and #Feminism tweets. *Feminist Media Studies*. (second round of revisions).

Gupta, S., Kaur, S., Gupta, M., & Singh, T. (2024). AI empowered academia: A fuzzy prioritization framework for academic challenges. *Journal of International Education in Business*, (October). https://doi.org/10.1108/jieb-06-2024-0071

Jemielniak, D. (2020). *Thick Big Data*. Oxford University Press.

Kakkar, V., Pandey, D. C., Verma, V., Mehrotra, R., Singh, P., & Tiwari, R. (2024). Artificial intelligence for stock prediction: A bibliometric review. In *2024 1st international conference on innovative sustainable technologies for energy, mechatronics, and smart systems (ISTEMS)* (pp. 1–5). IEEE.

Laxmi, B., Devi, P. U. M., Thanjavur, N., & Buddolla, V. (2024). The applications of artificial intelligence (AI)-driven tools in virus-like particles (VLPs) research. *Current Microbiology, 81*(8), 234.

Lorkowski, S. W., Dermawan, J. K., & Rubin, B. P. (2024). The practical utility of AI-assisted molecular profiling in the diagnosis and management of cancer of unknown primary: An updated review. *Virchows Archiv: An International Journal of Pathology, 484*(2), 369–375.

Lytras, M. D., Serban, A. C., Alkhaldi, A., Aldosemani, T., & Malik, S. (2024). What's next in higher education: The AI revolution 2030. In *Digital transformation in higher education, part A* (pp. 155–172). Emerald Publishing Limited.

Mahmoudi, A., Jemielniak, D., & Ciechanowski, L. (2024). Assessing accuracy: A study of Lexicon and rule-based packages in R and python for sentiment analysis. *IEEE Access: Practical Innovations, Open Solutions, 12*, 20169–20180.

Materia, S., García, L. P., van Straaten, C., Sungmin, A. M., Cavicchia, L., Coumou, D., de Luca, P., Kretschmer, M., & Donat, M. (2024). Artificial intelligence for climate prediction of extremes: State of the art, challenges, and future perspectives. *Wiley Interdisciplinary Reviews: Climate Change*, (September). https://doi.org/10.1002/wcc.914

Mohammed, T. J., Xinying, C., Alnoor, A., Khaw, K. W., Albahri, A. S., Teoh, W. L., Chong, Z. L., & Saha, S. (2024). A systematic review of artificial intelligence in orthopaedic disease detection: A taxonomy for analysis and trustworthiness evaluation. *International Journal of Computational Intelligence Systems, 17*(1). https://doi.org/10.1007/s44196-024-00718-y

Mohanty, S. S., Dash, S. R., & Parida, S. (Eds.). (2024). *Applying AI-based tools and technologies towards revitalization of indigenous and endangered languages* (2024th ed.). Springer.

Neff, T., & Jemielniak, D. (2022). How do transnational public spheres emerge? Comparing news and social media networks during the Madrid climate talks. *New Media & Society*, (March), 1461444822108126.

Prevedello, L. M., Halabi, S. S., Shih, G., Wu, C. C., Kohli, M. D., Chokshi, F. H., Erickson, B. J., Kalpathy-Cramer, J., Andriole, K. P., & Flanders, A. E. (2019). Challenges related to artificial intelligence research in medical imaging and the importance of image analysis competitions. *Radiology. Artificial Intelligence, 1*(1), e180031.

Rajpurkar, P., Chen, E., Banerjee, O., & Topol, E. J. (2022). AI in health and medicine. *Nature Medicine, 28*(1), 31–38.

Robledo, S., Aguirre, A. M. G., Hughes, M., & Eggers, F. (2021). 'Hasta La Vista, Baby' – Will machine learning terminate human literature reviews in entrepreneurship? *Journal of Small Business Management*, (August), 1–30.

Saleh, A., Sukaik, R., & Abu-Naser, S. S. (2020). Brain tumor classification using deep learning. In *2020 international conference on assistive and rehabilitation technologies (ICareTech)* (pp. 131–136). IEEE.

Sufi, F. K., & Khalil, I. (2024). Automated disaster monitoring from social media posts using AI-based location intelligence and sentiment analysis. *IEEE Transactions on Computational Social Systems, 11*(4), 4614–4624.

Szulc, N. A., Mackiewicz, Z., Bujnicki, J. M., & Stefaniak, F. (2023). Structural interaction fingerprints and machine learning for predicting and explaining binding of small molecule ligands to RNA. *Briefings in Bioinformatics, 24*(4). https://doi.org/10.1093/bib/bbad187

Thaichana, P., Oo, M. Z., Thorup, G. L., Chansakaow, C., Arworn, S., & Rerkasem, K. (2025). Integrating artificial intelligence in medical writing: Balancing technological innovation and human expertise, with practical applications in lower extremity wounds care. *The International Journal of Lower Extremity Wounds*, (January), 15347346241312814.

Zahra, W., & Rautela, G. (2024). Revolutionizing learning landscapes: Unleashing the potential of AI in the realm of academic research. In *Artificial intelligence: A multidisciplinary approach towards teaching and learning* (pp. 242–264). Bentham Science.

CHAPTER 8

Practical Tips and Resources

Abstract This chapter provides a practical guide to using generative AI in academia, offering strategies for integrating AI into research, teaching, and administrative workflows. It outlines foundational principles for effective AI use, including prompt engineering, critical evaluation of outputs, and tool selection based on context and discipline. The chapter emphasizes the importance of developing AI literacy—treating AI as a collaborator rather than a replacement—and provides guidance on navigating common limitations, such as hallucinations, citation errors, and shallow analysis. By cultivating adaptable AI skills and applying them thoughtfully, academics can enhance productivity, maintain scholarly integrity, and stay ahead in an evolving technological landscape.

Keywords AI literacy • Prompt engineering • Academic productivity • AI integration • Citation errors • Workflow automation • Research tools • Teaching with AI • Scholarly integrity • Academic administration

Generative AI has introduced a transformative shift in how academics approach research, writing, teaching, and administrative tasks (Dwivedi et al., 2023). While previous chapters have explored how AI can assist in drafting and refining academic work, this chapter expands on its broader applications. Beyond writing, AI can streamline workflows, assist in

E. Haber et al., *Using AI in Academic Writing and Research*, https://doi.org/10.1007/978-3-031-91705-9_8

research management, improve teaching strategies, and enhance efficiency in administrative duties. However, to fully harness the potential of AI, academics must develop proficiency in using these tools, critically evaluate their outputs, and integrate them thoughtfully into their work (Bockting et al., 2023).

This chapter offers a practical guide to using generative AI effectively in academia. It covers strategies for selecting and evaluating AI tools, developing AI literacy, and integrating AI into daily academic tasks. Additionally, we discuss the limitations and challenges that come with AI use, including common errors (Southworth et al., 2023), which will also be further discussed in Chap. 10. Since AI technology evolves rapidly, the focus here is not on specific tools but on general principles that will remain useful regardless of how the technology advances.

Understanding how to use AI effectively requires more than just familiarity with a particular model or platform. Just as early internet users had to navigate evolving search engines, today's academics must adapt to an AI landscape that is constantly changing. The key to long-term success lies in developing adaptable AI skills, critically assessing AI-generated content, and using these tools as collaborators rather than replacements for scholarly expertise.

STARTING WITH AI

We have already covered many aspects of generative AI in previous chapters, particularly in relation to drafting academic work. This chapter takes a broader approach, offering general guidance on how to effectively integrate generative AI into academic tasks beyond writing. We will explore its potential in research, teaching, and administrative work while also addressing how to evaluate and choose the best AI tools in an era of rapid technological advancement. With new models and platforms emerging constantly, knowing how to navigate this evolving landscape is essential for academics who want to make the most of these tools (Southworth et al., 2023).

The first step in effectively using AI is to become familiar with general-purpose generative AI tools. However, before diving into specific platforms, it is important to acknowledge a key limitation: everything we write here is subject to rapid change. Just as a book about the internet written in the early 1990s might have discussed search engines like Lycos or WebCrawler, by the early 2000s, such a guide would have been outdated, as Google and other advanced search tools became dominant. That being said, the core principles of how to use AI effectively should remain largely the same, even as the technology continues to evolve. The way we interact with generative AI—through prompts and iterative refinement—will likely remain central, even as the models themselves improve.

One of the most crucial skills in working with AI is prompt engineering. While we have touched on this before in Chap. 4, it is worth emphasizing again: the quality of AI-generated output is directly influenced by the precision of your prompts. If you do not understand what generative AI can and cannot do, you are likely to struggle with it, waste time, or receive poor results (Mollick & Mollick, 2023). To avoid this, we set a few basic rules (or principles) that will aid you in using generative AI more effectively in your academic (or any) work.

The first rule of using AI effectively is to be specific. Whether you are using ChatGPT (perhaps the "Lycos" of our time), Claude (the "WebCrawler"), or DeepSeek, you must clearly communicate what you need. Are you searching for relevant research? Brainstorming ideas? Drafting text? Evaluating student work? Each task requires a different approach, and AI tools cannot infer your exact needs unless you explicitly define them (Southworth et al., 2023).

This leads to a second fundamental principle: AI does not truly understand you or your content. Generative AI models are language models, not reasoning engines. They function based on statistical probabilities, predicting the most likely next word or phrase in response to your input. This means that while their answers may sound highly convincing, they are ultimately based on patterns in data, not genuine comprehension (Bockting et al., 2023). For example, when you ask AI to generate a research summary, it does not critically analyze sources the way a human would—it constructs a response based on existing linguistic structures and probabilities. This distinction is crucial to keep in mind, as it influences both the strengths and limitations of AI-assisted academic work.

BUILDING AI SKILLS

Building AI skills is much like learning to ride a bike. It can feel frustrating at first, especially if you don't follow the right techniques. As mentioned earlier, disappointment with initial results can lead to disengagement and missed opportunities to leverage AI effectively (Mollick & Mollick, 2023). Just as learning to cycle requires understanding balance, control, and movement, using generative AI requires mastering prompts, refining outputs, and recognizing its strengths and limitations. The key is to approach it as a skill that improves with practice.

This book provides a solid foundation, particularly for those comfortable with self-learning. However, practice is essential. The advice given here must be applied, tested, and adapted to fit your specific needs. As AI tools evolve rapidly, discipline-specific applications will continue to emerge, and while we cannot cover every new development, the core principles remain the same. If you engage with generative AI regularly and incorporate it into your academic routine, you will become increasingly proficient—just as riding a bike becomes second nature the more you practice (Southworth et al., 2023).

Beyond self-learning, it is valuable to seek additional training and resources. Many academic institutions now offer workshops, training programs, or online courses on AI for faculty and researchers (e.g., Cornell University, 2023). Universities are increasingly incorporating AI literacy into professional development, recognizing its growing role in research, teaching, and administration (Carvalho et al., 2022). Additionally, a wealth of publicly available resources exists, from YouTube tutorials to online courses and expert-led discussions. Like any evolving technology, staying informed and continuously refining your skills will help you use AI more effectively over time.

Developing and maintaining AI literacy is crucial for academics navigating an increasingly AI-driven world. This means not only understanding how to use generative AI but also critically assessing its outputs, recognizing potential biases, and staying updated on emerging tools and ethical considerations (Bockting et al., 2023). AI is not a static technology—it is constantly evolving. Those who invest time in learning, experimenting, and integrating AI into their workflows will be best positioned to harness its full potential. Just as digital literacy became an essential skill in academia with the rise of the internet, AI literacy is becoming equally indispensable (Southworth et al., 2023).

EVALUATING AI TOOLS

Evaluating AI tools requires an understanding of both general-purpose generative AI models and more specialized applications designed for academic work. While general AI models like ChatGPT, Claude, and Gemini continue to improve, they still have limitations, particularly when it comes to tasks that require access to proprietary databases, field-specific methodologies, or discipline-specific knowledge (Dwivedi et al., 2023). As AI advances, it is possible that these general-purpose tools will become more capable of handling specialized academic tasks, but for now, researchers often need to explore additional AI-driven platforms tailored to their specific needs (Van Dis et al., 2023).

Specialized AI tools can help bridge gaps where general-purpose models fall short. For instance, while ChatGPT can assist in summarizing concepts, it may not be sufficient for conducting a comprehensive literature review, as it lacks direct access to academic databases. This is where platforms like Elicit.org come in, allowing users to refine research questions, retrieve relevant papers, and analyze findings systematically (OECD, 2023). Another example is Undermind.ai, which acts as an AI-powered research assistant, scanning and summarizing large volumes of academic papers to provide researchers with deeper insights. These tools can significantly enhance efficiency, particularly in fields that rely on extensive literature analysis.

Some AI tools are even designed for highly specific disciplines. In law, for example, Harvey AI assists legal professionals with contract analysis, case law summarization, and legal research, streamlining workflows in ways that general AI models cannot. Similar discipline-specific AI applications are emerging across medicine, engineering, and the humanities, offering tailored support that aligns with the research needs of different academic communities (OECD, 2023).

Since the landscape of AI tools is evolving rapidly, there is no definitive list of platforms that every researcher should use. Instead, scholars must evaluate each tool individually, considering its usefulness within their own field and workflow (Bockting et al., 2023). Choosing the right tool is highly subjective—what works well for one researcher may not be effective for another. Testing different platforms and assessing their strengths and weaknesses is essential, but doing so requires a solid understanding of generative AI. Without a foundational grasp of how these tools operate, it is easy to overlook their limitations or misuse them, leading to suboptimal results.

To make the most of AI in academic work, researchers should stay informed about new developments, engage with AI-focused academic networks, and experiment with different tools to determine which best aligns with their needs (Van Noorden & Perkel, 2023). As with any emerging technology, proficiency comes with practice, and those who actively refine their AI literacy will be better positioned to leverage its full potential.

Integrating AI into Workflows

We have already explored how generative AI can enhance academic writing, grant proposals, and publishing, but its utility extends far beyond these tasks. Once you develop AI literacy, you can incorporate it into nearly every aspect of your academic workflow, streamlining both research and administrative responsibilities (Southworth et al., 2023). AI is not just a tool for writing—it can assist with brainstorming, automating repetitive tasks, improving communication, and optimizing time management (Bockting et al., 2023).

One immediate application is email management and communication. Academics receive a constant stream of emails—calls for papers, workshop invitations, administrative updates, journal announcements, and student inquiries. Managing these efficiently can be challenging. AI can help by summarizing long emails, allowing you to quickly grasp key points without reading every word (Mollick & Mollick, 2023). For instance, if you receive multiple announcements from various institutions, AI can extract only the most relevant information. You can also use AI to determine which opportunities are worth your attention by prompting: "Does this call for papers align with my research interests?" or "Summarize this conference invitation and highlight why it might be relevant for me."

Beyond reading emails more efficiently, AI can also draft responses, saving time while ensuring clarity and tone consistency. When composing an email, be specific about what you need. For instance, you can prompt AI to draft a kind response to a student request or a firm but professional reply to an editor. AI can even fine-tune tone adjustments, making a message 10 percent more polite or slightly more assertive. If you need to decline an invitation but wish to maintain a good relationship, AI can generate a response that is both appreciative and strategic. Similarly, for routine emails—such as scheduling meetings or responding to administrative inquiries—you can simply paste the email content into AI and ask it to draft a concise reply.

AI can also improve teaching and course management. It can assist in designing syllabi, generating lecture notes, and creating assessment rubrics (Carvalho et al., 2022). A particularly valuable application is exam creation. AI can help generate multiple-choice questions, short-answer prompts, or essay topics based on course material (Pomerlau, 2023). You can refine AI-generated questions to ensure they align with learning objectives, difficulty levels, and course themes. Additionally, AI can assist in grading, especially for structured assignments like multiple-choice exams or standardized assessments. For open-ended responses, AI can provide preliminary feedback, highlight key areas of improvement, and even suggest possible grading rubrics (Cornell Guidance, 2023). However, when using AI for grading, it is essential to review how it assessed student work and why. AI-generated grading suggestions should be cross-checked to ensure they align with academic expectations and do not introduce biases (Bockting et al., 2023).

In research management, AI can support literature tracking and organization, helping academics stay updated with the latest developments in their fields. AI-powered tools can summarize new publications, extract key findings, and highlight relevant trends (OECD, 2023). You can use AI to generate research summaries by pasting abstracts and asking for comparisons between multiple papers. It can also assist in structuring research projects by generating timelines, breaking down tasks, and offering recommendations for methodological approaches.

Beyond research and teaching, AI can streamline administrative tasks. Many academics juggle multiple responsibilities, from reviewing grant applications to organizing conferences and managing institutional reports (Southworth et al., 2023). AI can assist in drafting agendas, summarizing meeting notes, generating reports, or even automating parts of the peer review process by analyzing submission trends (Conroy, 2023). In time, institutions may integrate AI into internal systems to enhance efficiency across various academic functions (Van Noorden & Perkel, 2023).

The key to fully integrating AI into academic workflows is to experiment with different applications and assess where they add the most value. While AI can automate certain tasks, it is most effective when used as a collaborative tool—one that enhances efficiency without replacing critical thinking and decision-making. As AI tools continue to evolve, those who actively incorporate them into their daily work will find new ways to optimize productivity and free up time for higher-level intellectual pursuits (Van Dis et al., 2023).

DEALING WITH ERRORS

Generative AI offers significant advantages in academic work, but it also introduces several challenges that require careful attention. One of the most critical issues is hallucinations (discussed in Chap. 4), where AI generates false or misleading information that appears credible but is entirely fabricated (Van Dis et al., 2023). This is particularly problematic in academic writing when AI invents citations, misattributes sources, or provides incorrect data. If left unchecked, such errors can undermine the credibility of research and lead to the spread of misinformation.

Another limitation is the shallow or incomplete nature of AI-generated analysis. While AI can summarize content, it does not fully comprehend context, methodology, or the nuances of academic debates (Dwivedi et al., 2023). As a result, AI-generated summaries may oversimplify complex arguments or omit key details that are crucial for scholarly discussions. This issue becomes especially evident in literature reviews, where AI may prioritize frequently cited papers over innovative or field-transforming research, reinforcing existing academic hierarchies (Bockting et al., 2023).

AI can also introduce errors in quantitative tasks. When asked to perform calculations, retrieve statistical data, or analyze numerical trends, AI may generate incorrect figures, misapply formulas, or rely on outdated sources. This is due to the fact that generative AI models are not designed as reasoning engines; they predict text based on patterns rather than executing mathematical or statistical operations with precision (Mollick & Mollick, 2023). Academics relying on AI for empirical research must carefully verify numerical outputs against original datasets and reliable sources.

Another common issue is citation inaccuracy. AI tools often fabricate references, presenting them as real journal articles, books, or conference proceedings (Conroy, 2023). If an AI-generated reference appears plausible but does not actually exist, it can mislead researchers and compromise academic integrity. As we discussed in Chap. 4, even when AI retrieves real citations, it may alter details such as author names, publication years, or page numbers, requiring careful fact-checking. To mitigate this risk, researchers should cross-check citations in academic databases like Google Scholar, JSTOR, or PubMed before incorporating them into their work (Cornell AI Guidelines, 2023).

Being mindful of these potential errors is essential across all academic applications of AI. Whether drafting research papers, preparing teaching materials, or summarizing reports, scholars must critically assess AI-generated content rather than accepting it at face value. A best practice is to verify key details through original sources, consult multiple AI responses for consistency, and refine outputs through iterative engagement. By maintaining an active role in the research and writing process, academics can harness AI's benefits while avoiding the pitfalls of automation.

CONCLUSION

Generative AI is transforming academic work, offering new possibilities in research, writing, teaching, and administration. While it cannot replace critical thinking or scholarly rigor, it serves as a powerful tool that, when used effectively, enhances productivity and streamlines workflows. However, its benefits come with challenges that require careful navigation. AI literacy is crucial—understanding how these tools work, recognizing their limitations, and developing strategies for their effective use. AI is not a magic solution but a resource that requires thoughtful engagement. Scholars who experiment, refine their approach, and critically assess AI-generated content will maximize its potential.

Beyond writing, AI supports academic workflows, from literature reviews and grading to administrative tasks and research management. Yet, responsible use is essential—ensuring accuracy, avoiding over-reliance, and maintaining scholarly integrity. AI's outputs must be verified, as the technology can misinterpret information, hallucinate sources, and introduce errors. As AI evolves, its role in academia will grow. Those who actively engage with it and refine their AI skills will be at the forefront of this transformation. The key is not to resist AI but to integrate it strategically—leveraging its strengths while upholding the depth, originality, and integrity that define academic scholarship.

REFERENCES

Bockting, C. L., van Dis, E. A. M., van Rooij, R., Zuidema, W., & Bollen, J. (2023). Living guidelines for generative AI—Why scientists must oversee its use. *Nature, 622*(7984), 693–696. https://doi.org/10.1038/d41586-023-03266-1

Carvalho, L., Martinez-Maldonado, R., Tsai, Y., Markauskaite, L., & De Laat, M. (2022). How can we design for learning in an AI world? *Computers and Education: Artificial Intelligence, 3*, 100050. https://doi.org/10.1016/j.caeai.2022.100053

Conroy, G. (2023). How ChatGPT and other AI tools could disrupt scientific publishing. *Nature, 622*, 234–236. https://www.nature.com/articles/d41586-023-03144-w

Cornell University. (2023). *Generative AI in academic research: Perspectives and cultural norms.* https://research-and-innovation.cornell.edu/generative-ai-in-academic-research

Dwivedi, Y. K., Kshetri, N., Hughes, L., Slade, E. L., Jeyaraj, A., Kar, A. K., Baabdullah, A. M., Koohang, A., Raghavan, V., Ahuja, M., Albanna, H., Albashrawi, M. A., Al-Busaidi, A. S., Balakrishnan, J., Barlette, Y., Basu, S., Bose, I., Brooks, L., Buhalis, D., Carter, L., & Wright, R. (2023). "So what if ChatGPT wrote it?" Multidisciplinary perspectives on opportunities, challenges and implications of generative conversational AI for research, practice and policy. *International Journal of Information Management, 71*, 102642. https://doi.org/10.1016/j.ijinfomgt.2023.102642

Mollick, E., & Mollick, L. (2023). Assigning AI: Seven approaches for students, with prompts. *SSRN*. https://papers.ssrn.com/sol3/papers.cfm?abstract_id=4475995.

OECD. (2023). *Artificial intelligence in science: Challenges, opportunities and the future of research.* OECD Publishing. https://doi.org/10.1787/a8d820bd-en

Pomerlau, M. (2023). Integrating AI into college writing and communication courses. *Tech Style.* https://techstyle.lmc.gatech.edu/integrating-ai-into-college-writing-and-communication-classes

Southworth, J., Migliaccio, K., Glover, J., Glover, J., Reed, D., McCarty, C., Brendemuhl, J., & Thomas, A. (2023). Developing a model for AI across the curriculum: Transforming the higher education landscape via innovation in AI literacy. *Computers and Education: Artificial Intelligence, 4*, 100127. https://doi.org/10.1016/j.caeai.2023.100127

Van Dis, E. A., Bollen, J., Zuidema, W., van Rooij, R., & Bockting, C. L. (2023). ChatGPT: Five priorities for research. *Nature, 614*(7947), 224–226. https://doi.org/10.1038/d41586-023-00288-7

Van Noorden, R., & Perkel, J. M. (2023). AI and science: What 1,600 researchers think. *Nature, 621*(7980), 672–675. https://www.nature.com/articles/d41586-023-02980-0

CHAPTER 9

Navigating the Regulatory and Ethical Landscape of AI in Academia

Abstract This chapter examines the regulatory and ethical complexities surrounding the use of generative AI in academia. As AI tools increasingly influence research, teaching, and evaluation, scholars must navigate a fragmented and rapidly evolving legal landscape—including issues of data protection, intellectual property, and institutional compliance. The chapter highlights major legal risks, such as privacy violations under GDPR and copyright uncertainties tied to AI-generated content. It also addresses deeper ethical concerns, including AI's tendency to reinforce academic bias, its opacity, and its impact on authorship, originality, and student assessment. Drawing on examples from peer review, grant applications, and educational settings, this chapter underscores the need for transparent policies, critical engagement, and institutional guidance to ensure that generative AI is used responsibly. Rather than offering definitive answers, it equips academics with the conceptual and practical tools needed to balance innovation with scholarly integrity.

Keywords AI regulation • Academic integrity • Generative AI ethics • Copyright • Data protection • GDPR • Authorship • Peer review • Student assessment • Institutional compliance • Academic publishing • AI bias • AI transparency • Intellectual property • Academic policy

© The Author(s), under exclusive license to Springer Nature Switzerland AG 2025
E. Haber et al., *Using AI in Academic Writing and Research*,
https://doi.org/10.1007/978-3-031-91705-9_9

The integration of generative AI into academia presents profound legal and ethical challenges that researchers, educators, and institutions must now confront. These challenges are particularly complex because AI technology is evolving rapidly, while regulatory frameworks and institutional policies struggle to keep pace. Universities and publishers are developing guidelines, courts are issuing new rulings, and policymakers are debating how to balance AI's benefits with its risks (Jabotinsky & Sarel, 2024). Meanwhile, scholars at all career stages must navigate a shifting landscape of rules and expectations, often without clear guidance on what is permitted, advisable, or ethical.

This uncertainty raises a host of pressing questions: Are researchers allowed to use AI in their work, and if so, which tools are acceptable? Can AI-generated content be included in publications, and should its use be disclosed? If AI models have been trained on copyrighted academic materials, does this affect how researchers should engage with them (Lemley, 2024)? How can scholars ensure the accuracy and integrity of AI-generated content? What are the implications for student learning and assessment when AI can generate essays, analyze data, and solve complex problems? How should institutions define responsible AI use in research, teaching, and administrative work? Moreover, privacy concerns loom large, particularly when sensitive research data is processed through external AI systems. At a broader level, questions about academic authenticity arise in an era where AI-generated content can blur the boundaries of human intellectual effort (U.K. Intellectual Property Office, 2024).

The regulatory landscape surrounding generative AI is dynamic and fragmented. Different jurisdictions have taken varying approaches to AI governance, and institutional policies continue to evolve as universities grapple with best practices (European Commission, 2023). But before we explore the main regulatory challenges, it is important to emphasize that this chapter does not constitute legal advice. Researchers and students should always consult their institutional policies, legal counsel, or funding bodies for specific guidance tailored to their circumstances. Instead, this discussion provides a general overview of the key regulatory and ethical considerations shaping the use of AI in academia. Given the pace of change in this field, what is permissible today may be restricted tomorrow, and institutions may implement new requirements as AI capabilities expand.

Yet, not all concerns surrounding AI are purely legal. The ethical dilemmas raised by generative AI go far beyond compliance with data protection laws or copyright restrictions. These tools have the potential to reinforce biases present in training data, influencing research conclusions or marginalizing underrepresented perspectives (Bommasani et al., 2021). AI-generated content can introduce errors or misleading information, risking the propagation of inaccuracies in academic discourse (Cotton et al., 2024). In teaching and learning, the rise of AI-assisted writing tools raises fundamental questions about assessment fairness, critical thinking skills, and the role of human creativity in scholarly work (Dehouche, 2021). Ethical issues also extend to research methodology—if AI can generate literature reviews or synthesize arguments, does this standardize research approaches in a way that discourages intellectual originality? Additionally, questions of authorship, attribution, and transparency are becoming central as AI's role in academic work expands (Jabotinsky & Sarel, 2024).

This chapter explores both the legal and ethical dimensions of generative AI in academia. While it cannot offer definitive answers to all of these evolving challenges, it highlights the key considerations that scholars and institutions must grapple with. Rather than attempting to predict every regulatory change or institutional policy shift, this discussion focuses on the most urgent issues shaping AI's place in research, teaching, and academic publishing today. Understanding these issues is essential for anyone who seeks to engage with AI tools while upholding academic integrity, legal compliance, and ethical responsibility.

The Regulatory Challenges

The use of generative AI in academia raises complex legal and regulatory issues. Data protection laws, such as the General Data Protection Regulation (GDPR) in the EU, impose strict requirements when AI tools process personal data. Intellectual property concerns complicate questions of ownership, copyright, and the legality of AI training datasets. Academic integrity policies increasingly mandate transparency in AI-assisted research and writing. Additionally, contractual obligations with publishers and licensing restrictions on AI tools shape how these technologies can be used in academic settings. As institutions and regulators adapt to AI's growing role, scholars must navigate an evolving landscape of legal and ethical constraints.

Data Protection and Privacy

The use of generative AI in academic research raises privacy and data protection concerns, particularly given that many AI tools process user inputs on external servers. This means that anything entered into an AI system could potentially be stored, analyzed, or even used for future model training unless explicitly stated otherwise (Ye et al., 2024). Researchers handling sensitive information, including personal data, confidential manuscripts, or unpublished findings, must take extra precautions to ensure compliance with data protection regulations and institutional policies. Without adequate safeguards, there is a risk that sensitive information could be inadvertently exposed, misused, or accessed by unauthorized parties (European Data Protection Supervisor, 2023).

One of the primary legal frameworks governing data protection is the GDPR, which applies in the EU and influences data privacy standards worldwide. Under GDPR, any processing of personal data must be conducted lawfully, fairly, and transparently (van Ooijen & Vrabec, 2019). If researchers use AI tools to process identifiable information, they must ensure a legal basis for doing so, particularly when dealing with human subject research. This applies not only to participant data but also to institutional research that may be subject to confidentiality agreements. Transferring identifiable personal data to external AI platforms without explicit consent could constitute a violation of data protection laws, even if no direct misuse occurs.

To mitigate these risks, researchers should use AI models that explicitly guarantee privacy protections. Many general-purpose AI tools store user inputs by default, especially free versions. For example, the free-tier version of ChatGPT retains conversations and may use them for training future models, whereas ChatGPT Enterprise does not store user inputs. Similarly, some academic AI tools provide explicit assurances that data will not be retained. Before using any AI tool, researchers should review the platform's privacy settings and, where necessary, directly ask whether the model retains data or uses it for training. Some AI providers allow users to disable data storage or history, but these settings are often not enabled by default.

For research involving sensitive or unpublished data, anonymization can serve as a safeguard, but it is not a foolproof solution. Instead of entering full research descriptions or participant details, placeholders or pseudonyms can be used to remove identifying information. However, AI models can infer missing details based on context, and when cross-referenced with other sources, even partially anonymized data can sometimes be re-identified (Wachter & Mittelstadt, 2019). If researchers are handling particularly sensitive datasets, avoiding cloud-based AI models altogether and opting for local AI tools may be the best approach. Some universities and research institutions are now developing sandboxed AI environments that allow researchers to use AI tools without transmitting data to external servers (Masso et al., 2025).

Beyond individual researcher choices, transparency is essential when AI tools are used in research involving human subjects. If AI assists in any form of data processing or analysis, informed consent documents should clearly disclose this. A properly structured consent form might state: *"This study utilizes AI-assisted tools to analyze anonymized data. No personal identifiers will be processed, and all information will remain confidential. The AI model used does not retain data or contribute to future training."* As institutional policies continue to evolve, many ethics committees and Institutional Review Boards (IRBs) are increasing their scrutiny of AI's role in handling research data. Some require researchers to explicitly disclose whether AI tools were used in data analysis, transcription, or any other aspect of research workflows. Failing to comply with these requirements may lead to ethical or regulatory violations, particularly for projects involving vulnerable populations, classified research, or international collaborations subject to multiple data protection regimes.

Data security is another critical consideration beyond anonymization. Unlike traditional research software, which allows users to control data storage and processing, many AI tools operate on proprietary cloud infrastructures where information may be accessed by the provider. This makes it difficult to ensure that sensitive information remains protected from unauthorized access or misuse. One potential solution for researchers working with confidential data is to use self-hosted AI models—large language models that run on local servers or institutional networks without transmitting data externally. Examples include open-source models such as LLaMA, Falcon, and Mistral, which can be fine-tuned and deployed within secure computing environments. Some universities are investing in private AI infrastructures, allowing faculty to use AI tools while ensuring that data does not leave institutional control.

Researchers handling proprietary, classified, or unpublished research should also be mindful of how AI tools manage temporary data storage. Some platforms retain session data for operational purposes, even if they do not use it for training. Checking whether the AI provider retains logs or transcripts is crucial before entering sensitive material. In some cases, contractual agreements—such as Data Processing Agreements (DPAs) under GDPR—can provide additional legal assurances that data will not be stored or shared with third parties.

By taking these precautions—reviewing AI privacy settings, avoiding the input of identifiable or unpublished data, using anonymization carefully, selecting tools with strict privacy protections, and ensuring transparency in informed consent—researchers can mitigate risks while benefiting from AI's capabilities. Given the rapidly evolving nature of AI governance, staying updated on institutional policies, legal frameworks, and best practices will be essential for the responsible use of AI in academic research.

Intellectual Property Considerations in Academic Use of Generative AI

The integration of generative AI into academic research and writing presents significant intellectual property (IP) challenges. Unlike traditional research tools, generative AI can generate substantial portions of text, summarize existing literature, and even assist in structuring arguments. These capabilities create complex questions about authorship, ownership, and attribution—issues that are becoming increasingly relevant as academic institutions and legal frameworks struggle to keep pace with AI's rapid development. While broader debates continue over whether training AI on copyrighted materials constitutes infringement (Lemley, 2024), this section focuses on the intellectual property issues that researchers, educators, and students face when using generative AI in academic settings.

One of the primary concerns is whether a researcher using generative AI retains full ownership of the resulting text. Copyright law generally assumes that only human authors can claim intellectual property rights, which complicates matters when AI significantly contributes to content creation. In the United States, the Copyright Office has ruled that purely AI-generated works are ineligible for copyright protection (U.S. Copyright Office, 2025). However, **AI-assisted works can be protected if there is sufficient human control and creative input**, but this determination is made on a case-by-case basis (U.S. Copyright Office, 2025). The key challenge is defining what constitutes creative human input. If a researcher drafts a paper with AI assistance but substantially revises and refines the content, ensuring that the arguments, analysis, and conclusions are their own, this is likely considered human authorship. However, if AI plays a dominant role in structuring the work or synthesizing information, the extent to which it remains "original" under copyright law becomes more ambiguous.

This issue is particularly relevant in collaborative research projects where multiple authors contribute to a paper. If one researcher heavily relies on AI while others do not, how should this be disclosed? Some academic publishers now require authors to state whether AI tools were used in drafting an article, while others explicitly prohibit listing AI as a co-author. The latter reflects the principle that authorship implies responsibility for the content, and since AI cannot be held accountable, it cannot be considered an author (Lemley, 2024). However, these policies do not resolve the broader question of how much AI use is acceptable before an academic's role in authorship is diminished. As institutions and publishers develop clearer policies, researchers must stay informed about evolving guidelines and ensure that their contributions remain intellectually significant.

This is where it is worth mentioning Ethan Mollick's concept of "co-intelligence," which frames AI as a collaborator rather than a replacement for human authorship (Mollick, 2024). Under this model, AI enhances efficiency and creativity but does not assume the role of a primary author. This approach aligns with how many academics currently use AI—refining drafts, suggesting alternative arguments, and improving clarity, rather than generating entire papers without oversight. If AI is used in this co-intelligence framework, transparency becomes crucial. Researchers should document how AI was involved in their work, distinguishing AI-generated inputs from their own intellectual contributions. Clear documentation can help prevent disputes over authorship, particularly in collaborative projects where different contributors may use AI to varying degrees.

To safeguard their intellectual contributions, researchers should maintain draft versions that show how AI-generated content was modified. By refining AI-generated text to reflect their own reasoning and ensuring that key arguments remain original, scholars can minimize the risk of AI overshadowing their authorship (Lemley, 2024). Institutions and research groups should also establish internal guidelines on AI use in collaborative projects, defining when and how AI contributions should be disclosed.

Beyond text, generative AI is increasingly being used to create figures, graphs, and conceptual diagrams for academic publications. While this provides an efficient and cost-effective way to generate visual content, it also introduces copyright risks. Some AI-generated images may closely resemble existing copyrighted material, raising concerns about unintentional infringement (U.S. Copyright Office, 2025). Researchers should carefully verify that AI-generated visuals do not replicate protected works, particularly when using tools that generate images based on large datasets of existing media. Some publishers now require authors to confirm that any AI-generated figures comply with copyright standards. Since many AI tools place the burden of ensuring originality on the user, researchers should take steps to verify compliance, such as running AI-generated images through reverse image searches or using copyright verification tools.

To mitigate the risk of copyright infringement, researchers should select AI tools carefully. Platforms trained on open-access datasets may be less likely to generate infringing content. Additionally, where possible, researchers can use AI tools that allow them to train models on their own datasets rather than relying on general-purpose models with unknown sources (Lemley, 2024). This approach reduces the likelihood of inadvertent copyright violations and provides more control over the data used to generate content.

Beyond copyright, generative AI use in research also raises concerns about patents and trade secrets. Many AI tools operate on cloud-based platforms, meaning that any information entered into them could potentially be stored, processed, or used for future model training. If a researcher inputs novel research findings, hypotheses, or experimental data into an AI system, this information could be accessed or inadvertently exposed. This has serious implications for patents, as public disclosure of an invention before filing a patent application can render it unpatentable in many jurisdictions (U.S. Copyright Office, 2025). Fields that rely heavily on intellectual property protection—such as biotechnology, engineering, and software development—should be particularly cautious when using generative AI in early-stage research.

To protect patentable research, scholars should avoid inputting unpublished findings into AI systems unless they are certain that the tool does not store or use their inputs for training. Some AI platforms now offer enterprise or academic versions that guarantee data privacy and security. Where possible, researchers should prioritize these versions over free, publicly available models. Additionally, institutions should develop best practices for AI-assisted research, ensuring that faculty and students understand the risks associated with disclosing sensitive information to AI models (U.S. Copyright Office, 2025).

Even when intellectual property rights are not at stake, generative AI presents challenges in maintaining originality in academic work. While copyright law does not protect ideas themselves, it does protect the specific expression of those ideas. If AI is used to generate summaries, arguments, or conceptual frameworks, there is a risk that multiple users working on similar topics may receive outputs that resemble one another. Since AI generates text based on patterns in existing works, its responses may reflect conventional phrasing, leading to concerns about the homogenization of academic writing. If many researchers rely on AI to summarize literature or structure arguments, academic discourse could become more uniform, with fewer distinctive writing styles or novel interpretations.

Institutions, funding bodies, and publishers are beginning to introduce clearer policies on AI use in academic research. Some universities require faculty to disclose whether AI was used in grant applications, research proposals, or publications submitted for institutional review. Similarly, funding agencies may implement policies to ensure that AI-assisted research meets ethical and legal standards. Researchers should stay informed about these evolving guidelines and ensure that their use of AI aligns with institutional and professional expectations.

As courts continue to address how copyright law applies to AI-generated content, the legal landscape may shift. Until clearer regulations emerge, scholars should take a cautious approach to integrating AI into their work. By documenting AI usage, verifying originality, and ensuring compliance with intellectual property laws, researchers can maximize the benefits of AI while avoiding potential legal pitfalls.

Compliance Essentials

Compliance with AI usage in academia goes beyond intellectual property and data protection. Much of it depends on institutional requirements, journal submission guidelines, and grant proposal regulations. Unlike legal frameworks, which are relatively established, institutional policies on AI are still evolving, making it crucial for researchers to stay updated on the specific rules that apply to their work.

One of the first considerations is university policies. Many academic institutions are in the process of defining their stance on AI-assisted research and writing. Some universities now require explicit disclosures when AI is used in drafting research papers, grant applications, or teaching materials, while others impose restrictions on AI-generated content, particularly in student assessments. Before incorporating AI into academic work, researchers should check their institution's official policies or consult with relevant faculty committees. In some cases, failing to disclose AI use—especially in high-stakes applications like grant proposals—could lead to ethical concerns or administrative complications.

Funding agencies are also adapting their regulations in response to AI's growing role in research. Some grant providers now require applicants to state whether AI was used in drafting proposals, conducting preliminary analyses, or reviewing literature. Others may impose stricter limitations, particularly for projects dealing with classified information, sensitive data, or regulatory compliance. Given that grant applications undergo rigorous scrutiny, failing to align with an agency's policies could jeopardize funding opportunities. Before submitting proposals, researchers should carefully review the specific guidelines of each funding body to ensure AI use falls within permitted boundaries.

Academic publishers are another key consideration. Many journals are actively updating their editorial policies to address the role of AI in scholarly writing. Some require authors to disclose whether AI-assisted drafting was involved, while others prohibit listing AI as a co-author, reinforcing the principle that human authors must take responsibility for the content. Some might ban any use of generative AI, or restrict it in another way. Additionally, journals may regulate the use of AI-generated figures, graphs, or images, particularly if these raise concerns about originality or copyright infringement. Before submitting a manuscript, authors should review the journal's policies to determine whether AI-generated content must be declared and whether specific restrictions apply. Ignoring these guidelines could lead to delays, rejections, ethical, and even legal concerns.

Beyond research and publishing, AI policies are also emerging in academic conferences and peer review processes. Some conferences have begun specifying whether AI-generated abstracts, proposals, or presentations are permitted. While AI tools can be useful for refining arguments and improving clarity, some academic organizations have raised concerns about the overuse of AI in submissions. Similarly, the use of AI in peer review remains controversial—some reviewers use AI to summarize papers, but many academic bodies discourage its use for evaluating submissions, as it could introduce biases or oversimplifications. Understanding these emerging norms is essential for researchers who frequently engage in peer review or conference participation.

To navigate these evolving policies, researchers should take a proactive approach. Before using AI in research, writing, or teaching, they should check for any institutional guidance, journal policies, or funding restrictions. If policies are unclear, seeking clarification from department heads, legal offices, or journal editors can prevent future complications. When in doubt, transparency is the best approach—disclosing AI use where required and maintaining human oversight in critical aspects of academic work ensures both compliance and research integrity.

Ethical Considerations and Challenges

The ethical dimensions of generative AI in academia extend beyond legal compliance and institutional policies, challenging long-standing norms of authorship, intellectual labor, and fairness in scholarly work (Jabotinsky & Sarel, 2024). Many academics, especially those encountering these tools for the first time, experience ethical uncertainty—some even liken AI-assisted writing to "cheating" (Dwivedi et al., 2023). This reaction is understandable. Academic traditions emphasize individual intellectual effort, and scholars are trained to carefully attribute sources when building on existing ideas. Now, generative AI can assist with everything from drafting sentences to suggesting theoretical frameworks, raising fundamental questions about the boundaries of original thinking and intellectual contribution.

However, framing AI use in binary terms—ethical versus unethical—is an oversimplification. The more pressing ethical challenges arise not from the mere use of AI, but from issues embedded in how AI models function. These include biases in training data, the opaque nature of AI-generated responses, and the risk of over-reliance (Dwivedi et al., 2023). These challenges demand a nuanced and critical approach when integrating AI into academic work.

One of the most significant ethical concerns is bias. AI models are trained on vast datasets composed of human-created content, inevitably inheriting the biases present in those sources (Jabotinsky & Sarel, 2024). As a result, generative AI can reinforce academic inequalities by disproportionately citing well-known scholars and prestigious institutions while marginalizing less visible research. This issue is particularly troubling in academia, where intellectual diversity and engagement with a broad range of perspectives are crucial to advancing knowledge.

For example, when asked to summarize research on a given topic, AI tools might prioritize widely cited papers rather than selecting the most innovative or field-transforming work (Dwivedi et al., 2023). This tendency reinforces existing academic hierarchies—further entrenching dominant voices while making it more difficult for emerging or less institutionally recognized scholars to gain visibility. The problem extends beyond citations. AI's reliance on past patterns means it tends to produce conventional interpretations rather than generating new insights. This could lead to a stagnation of academic discourse, where scholars rely on AI-generated summaries that merely recycle prevailing perspectives rather than challenging existing paradigms.

This bias has particularly significant implications for early-career researchers and scholars from underrepresented regions or disciplines (Jabotinsky & Sarel, 2024). If AI-assisted research tools continue to prioritize highly cited works from dominant academic hubs, it will become even harder for alternative voices to gain recognition. While AI may accelerate research efficiency, it also risks reinforcing the status quo rather than fostering the kind of intellectual diversity that is essential for scholarly progress. To counteract this, researchers must remain vigilant in supplementing AI-generated references with their own exploration of the literature, ensuring that their engagement with academic sources remains critical, inclusive, and comprehensive.

Beyond research bias, AI's lack of transparency presents another ethical challenge. Many generative AI models operate as black boxes, meaning users do not fully understand why an AI model produces a particular response, what sources it is drawing from, or whether external factors influence its outputs (Jabotinsky & Sarel, 2024). This opacity is especially problematic in academic research, where transparency and reproducibility are fundamental principles. Scholars must be able to trace the origins of their sources and justify their conclusions—but AI-generated content lacks the clear citation structures and methodological explanations that traditional research practices require.

For instance, some AI models impose content restrictions or modify responses based on pre-programmed safeguards. This can be politically or ideologically motivated (Dwivedi et al., 2023). A striking example occurred with DeepSeek, a Chinese-developed AI model, which provided vague or censored responses when queried about historical events in China. Such cases illustrate how AI's outputs can be subtly shaped by non-academic considerations, making it imperative that scholars critically evaluate AI-generated material rather than accepting it at face value. Given that researchers may not always know which biases are embedded in a model, it is essential to approach AI-generated research suggestions with scrutiny, cross-checking claims with verified sources.

Generative AI also raises ethical concerns in academic teaching and assessment. AI's role in education is expanding, and while it can be a valuable tool for personalized learning, grading automation, and curriculum development, it must be used with caution to preserve academic integrity. One of the most pressing concerns is the increasing reliance of students on AI-generated essays, assignments, and even exam responses (Dwivedi et al., 2023). This trend poses a dilemma for educators: should AI-generated content be strictly prohibited, or should students be encouraged to use AI responsibly, with clear guidelines on when and how it is appropriate?

A possible solution lies in ethical AI literacy—teaching students not just how to use AI but how to engage with it critically (Jabotinsky & Sarel, 2024). Instead of outright bans, universities could require students to disclose AI assistance in their work, much like citing sources in traditional research. This approach acknowledges AI's role as a legitimate tool while preventing deceptive practices. However, such policies must be carefully crafted to avoid creating undue burdens for students or faculty, particularly in institutions where AI literacy resources are not widely available.

Another concern is the potential erosion of students' critical thinking and writing skills if they become overly dependent on AI. If students routinely rely on AI to structure arguments or generate insights, they may fail to develop the intellectual rigor necessary for deep academic engagement (Dwivedi et al., 2023). To address this, educators should design assessments that require original thought and active participation—oral exams, handwritten assignments, and AI-free in-class discussions are possible ways to ensure that students continue developing essential analytical skills.

Universities and academic publishers are beginning to respond to these ethical concerns by establishing clearer policies on AI use (Jabotinsky & Sarel, 2024). As mentioned, some journals now require authors to disclose whether AI-assisted writing was used in an article, while others prohibit listing AI as a co-author to reinforce the principle that authors must be accountable for their work. Similarly, funding agencies are increasingly requiring transparency regarding AI use in grant proposals. These emerging policies signal a growing institutional recognition that AI is reshaping academic work, and researchers must adapt to evolving standards.

Ultimately, generative AI is neither an unequivocal benefit nor an inherent threat to academic integrity. Its impact depends on how it is used. If scholars remain critically engaged—recognizing AI's limitations, questioning its biases, and supplementing its outputs with rigorous research—then these tools can serve as valuable assistants rather than sources of ethical concern. However, failing to address these challenges could lead to an academic landscape in which AI not only accelerates research but also distorts it, reinforcing existing inequalities and weakening the foundational principles of scholarly inquiry. By approaching AI with skepticism, ethical awareness, and an emphasis on human expertise, academia can harness AI's potential while safeguarding the values that define intellectual progress.

AI in Academic Evaluation: Challenges and Best Practices for Peer Review, Grant Assessment, and Student Evaluation

The integration of AI into academic evaluation processes—ranging from peer review and grant evaluations to student assessment—raises complex questions about fairness, bias, transparency, and accountability. While AI can streamline these processes, enhance efficiency, and provide valuable insights, it also introduces risks that must be carefully managed to maintain academic integrity.

AI's role in peer review is particularly contentious. While peer review remains a cornerstone of academic publishing, it is also an imperfect and time-consuming process, subject to human biases and inconsistencies. AI-assisted tools have been proposed as a way to alleviate some of these burdens. They can summarize manuscripts, highlight key arguments, identify methodological flaws, and flag potential ethical concerns, helping reviewers assess submissions more efficiently. Some tools even compare new manuscripts against existing literature to detect novelty, redundancy, or potential plagiarism. However, AI's capacity to perform these tasks objectively is limited. It operates based on statistical patterns and linguistic probability rather than deep comprehension, making it prone to missing nuanced theoretical contributions or methodological innovations.

Moreover, AI-assisted review tools may reinforce existing academic hierarchies rather than promote fair evaluation. Since generative AI models are trained on past academic outputs, they tend to mirror established citation patterns and institutional biases, favoring research from prestigious universities or high-impact journals while overlooking lesser-known but equally valuable contributions. This raises concerns about fairness and diversity in academic publishing. If AI is incorporated into peer review, journals and publishers must ensure that its use does not inadvertently reinforce structural biases. Transparency is crucial: if AI is used to generate review summaries or recommendations, reviewers should be aware of how these tools influence their evaluations. AI should not replace the essential task of critical scholarly judgment, nor should it be used as an unquestioned authority in manuscript assessment.

A similar set of challenges arises when AI is used in grant evaluations. Funding agencies are beginning to explore AI's role in streamlining the review of research proposals. AI can be used to check compliance with funding guidelines, identify potential conflicts of interest, and compare proposals against existing funded projects. In theory, this could make grant evaluations more systematic and less susceptible to personal biases. However, as with peer review, AI-driven evaluation tools can introduce new concerns. If trained on historical funding decisions, AI models may replicate past biases, reinforcing existing disparities in research funding distribution. Certain disciplines, methodologies, or institutions may be systematically favored over others, limiting opportunities for innovative or unconventional research. Furthermore, the qualitative aspects of grant evaluation—such as assessing a project's potential impact, originality, and feasibility—require human judgment that AI cannot fully replicate. To ensure fairness, funding agencies should treat AI-generated evaluations as advisory rather than determinative, allowing applicants to contest assessments where necessary and maintaining human oversight in final funding decisions.

Beyond academic publishing and grant allocation, AI is increasingly being used in student assessment and exam evaluation. AI tools can assist educators in grading essays, evaluating exam responses, and providing feedback on student work. For structured assessments, such as multiple-choice tests, AI-driven grading can offer significant efficiency gains. For open-ended assignments, AI tools can analyze grammar, coherence, and even argument structure, providing preliminary evaluations that instructors can refine. AI also has potential in formative assessment, where it can generate immediate feedback for students, helping them identify areas for improvement before submitting final work.

However, the limitations of AI in assessment cannot be overlooked. AI cannot fully evaluate originality, depth of analysis, or critical thinking—qualities that are central to higher education. If overused, AI grading tools risk reducing student evaluations to surface-level pattern recognition rather than genuine engagement with student work. Moreover, AI's reliance on past data means that it may reinforce dominant discourse structures, penalizing unconventional thinking or creative approaches that do not conform to expected patterns. In disciplines that value argumentation and interpretative nuance, AI's grading capabilities remain questionable at best.

AI's role in exam construction also raises important pedagogical considerations. AI can generate multiple-choice questions, essay prompts, and even case study scenarios based on course materials. While this can be a useful starting point, instructors must ensure that AI-generated assessments align with learning objectives and do not merely test recall of information. AI can also assist in analyzing past exams to identify areas where students struggle, helping educators refine their teaching strategies. However, reliance on AI-generated exams without careful human review risks producing superficial or repetitive assessments that fail to measure deeper learning outcomes.

Academic integrity is another major concern. As AI tools become more sophisticated, students have increasing access to AI-generated assistance for assignments and exams. This poses challenges for educators seeking to ensure fair assessment practices. Traditional plagiarism detection tools are not always effective in identifying AI-generated content, raising questions about how institutions should address AI-assisted academic work. Some universities are beginning to require students to disclose the use of AI in their assignments, similar to citing sources in conventional research. While this approach promotes transparency, it also raises the question of how much AI assistance is acceptable. If AI helps refine sentence structure but does not generate substantive content, should this be disclosed? If AI suggests an entire argument framework, does that constitute an undue advantage? These issues will likely require new academic policies and a shift in how originality is assessed in student work.

Rather than outright prohibitions on AI use, institutions may benefit from promoting ethical AI literacy among students. Teaching students how to use AI as a supplementary tool—rather than as a substitute for original thinking—can help prevent academic misconduct while still allowing students to benefit from AI's capabilities. Educators should design assessments that emphasize analytical engagement, such as in-class writing, oral examinations, and assignments that require iterative drafting with feedback. These approaches can help ensure that students develop critical thinking and writing skills rather than relying passively on AI-generated content.

As AI becomes more integrated into peer review, grant evaluation, and student assessment, institutions must establish clear guidelines to ensure that its use enhances rather than undermines academic integrity. Transparency is key: scholars, students, and reviewers must understand how AI is being used and where its limitations lie. While AI can assist in these processes, it should not replace human judgment, nor should its outputs be treated as definitive assessments of academic quality. By maintaining oversight, fostering AI literacy, and designing evaluation methods that prioritize critical engagement, academia can leverage AI's benefits while upholding the standards of fairness, originality, and scholarly rigor.

Conclusion

The integration of generative AI into academia presents both opportunities and challenges, requiring scholars, institutions, and policymakers to navigate an evolving legal, ethical, and practical landscape. As AI tools become more sophisticated, they will increasingly shape how research is conducted, how academic writing is produced, how students learn, and how scholarly work is evaluated. Yet, these advancements also bring risks that must be addressed—intellectual property uncertainties, data privacy concerns, biases embedded in AI-generated content, and the potential erosion of critical thinking and originality in academic work.

Regulatory frameworks, institutional policies, and professional norms are still adapting to the rapid development of AI. While existing laws governing intellectual property, data protection, and academic integrity provide some guidance, they do not yet fully account for the complexities introduced by generative AI. Researchers and educators must remain proactive in understanding how these evolving legal and institutional requirements apply to their work, ensuring compliance with privacy laws, IP protections, and institutional disclosure policies. Transparency will be key, particularly in contexts where AI plays a significant role in drafting, analysis, or decision-making.

Beyond legal compliance, ethical considerations must remain central to AI's use in academia. Issues such as bias in AI-generated content, the opacity of AI decision-making, and the fairness of AI-assisted student evaluation require critical engagement. While AI can accelerate research, improve efficiency, and provide valuable analytical support, it should not become a substitute for human judgment, creativity, or intellectual rigor. Scholars must critically assess AI-generated outputs, cross-check sources, and ensure that AI is used as a tool to enhance—not replace—academic expertise.

For institutions, the challenge will be to craft policies that strike a balance between innovation and academic integrity. Universities must develop clear guidelines on AI's role in research, teaching, and evaluation, ensuring that AI literacy becomes a core part of academic training. Similarly, academic publishers and funding bodies must refine their policies to address AI's growing role in scholarly work, maintaining high standards for authorship, attribution, and research ethics.

Ultimately, generative AI is neither an existential threat nor a guaranteed benefit to academia—it is a powerful tool whose impact depends on how it is integrated. By approaching AI with critical awareness, ethical responsibility, and a commitment to academic integrity, scholars can harness its potential while safeguarding the values that underpin scholarly inquiry. The future of AI in academia will not be shaped solely by technological advancements but by the choices institutions and individuals make in adopting, regulating, and refining its use.

REFERENCES

Bommasani, R., Hudson, D. A., Adeli, E., Altman, R., Arora, S., von Arx, S., Bernstein, M. S., Bohg, J., Bosselut, A., Brunskill, E., Brynjolfsson, E., Buch, S., Cardie, C., Catanzaro, B., Chang, K. W., Clark, J., Conneau, A., Darrell, T., ... Liang, P. (2021). *On the opportunities and risks of foundation models.* arXiv preprint arXiv:2108.07258.

Cotton, D. R. E., Cotton, P. A., & Shipway, J. R. (2024). Chatting and cheating: Ensuring academic integrity in the era of ChatGPT. *Innovations in Education and Teaching International, 61*(2), 228–239. https://doi.org/10.1080/14703297.2023.2190148

Dehouche, N. (2021). Plagiarism in the age of massive Generative Pre-trained Transformers (GPT-3). *International Journal for Educational Integrity, 17*(1), 1–12. https://doi.org/10.1007/s40979-021-00070-5

Dwivedi, Y. K., Kshetri, N., Hughes, L., Slade, E. L., Jeyaraj, A., Kar, A. K., & Wright, R. (2023). "So what if ChatGPT wrote it?" Multidisciplinary perspectives on opportunities, challenges, and implications of generative conversational AI for research, practice, and policy. *International Journal of Information Management, 71*, 102642. https://doi.org/10.1016/j.ijinfomgt.2023.102642

European Data Protection Supervisor. (2023). *EDPS guidelines on generative AI: Embracing opportunities, protecting people.* European Union Publications. https://www.edps.europa.eu/press-publications/press-news/press-releases/2024/edps-guidelines-generative-ai-embracing-opportunities-protecting-people_en

Jabotinsky, H. Y., & Sarel, R. (2024). Co-authoring with an AI? Ethical dilemmas and artificial intelligence. *Arizona State Law Journal, 56*(1), 188–202.

Lemley, M. A. (2024). How generative AI turns copyright law upside down. *Columbia Science & Technology Law Review, 25*(1), 190–212.

Masso, A., Gerassimenko, J., Kasapoglu, T., & Beilmann, M. (2025). Research ethics committees as knowledge gatekeepers: The impact of emerging technologies on social science research. *Journal of Responsible Technology, 21*, 100112. https://doi.org/10.1016/j.jrt.2025.100112

Mollick, E. (2024). *Co-intelligence: Living and working with AI.* Portfolio/Penguin.

U.K. Intellectual Property Office. (2024). *Artificial intelligence and copyright: Consultation and policy recommendations.* https://www.gov.uk/government/consultations/copyrigh-and-artificial-intelligence/copyright-and-artificial-intelligence

U.S. Copyright Office. (2025). *Copyright and artificial intelligence: Part 2 – Copyrightability report.* U.S. Copyright Office. https://www.copyright.gov/ai/Copyright-and-Artificial-Intelligence-Part-2-Copyrightability-Report.pdf

van Ooijen, I., & Vrabec, H. U. (2019). Does the GDPR enhance consumers' control over personal data? An analysis from a behavioural perspective. *Journal of Consumer Policy, 42*(1), 91–107. https://doi.org/10.1007/s10603-018-9399-7

Wachter, S., & Mittelstadt, B. (2019). A right to reasonable inferences: Re-thinking data protection law in the age of AI. *Columbia Law Review, 119*(5), 1301–1369.

Ye, F., Li, T., & Zhang, X. (2024). AI-driven data governance: Analyzing privacy risks and mitigation strategies. *Computers & Law, 41*(2), 91–109.

CHAPTER 10

Conclusions: The Dawn of Generative AI in Academia

Abstract This concluding chapter reflects on the transformative impact of generative AI on academic research, writing, teaching, and institutional practice. Rather than treating AI as a mere tool for efficiency, it considers how AI is reshaping foundational aspects of scholarly work, from research methodology to authorship, peer review, and pedagogy. The chapter argues that generative AI represents a paradigmatic shift in knowledge production, requiring scholars to rethink traditional norms of intellectual labor, originality, and disciplinary boundaries. It explores both the opportunities and the ethical challenges that come with integrating AI into academia, including questions of bias, equity, sustainability, and academic integrity. Emphasizing the concept of collaborative AI, it advocates for a vision in which human creativity and ethical judgment work alongside machine intelligence to advance scholarship. The chapter concludes by calling for critical engagement, institutional responsibility, and collective reflection, urging academia to shape the future of AI integration in a way that strengthens, rather than compromises, its core mission.

Keywords Generative AI • Academic transformation • Research methodology • Scholarly authorship • Academic integrity • AI ethics • Collaborative AI • Epistemology • Interdisciplinary research • Academic publishing • Higher education policy • AI literacy • Academic governance • Sustainability • Technological change

The academic world now finds itself simultaneously embracing and questioning these powerful new tools. Researchers who once spent weeks conducting literature reviews can now generate comprehensive syntheses in hours. Scholars struggling with writer's block can engage with AI systems that suggest alternative phrasings, structures, and arguments. Students are experimenting with new forms of learning and knowledge creation facilitated by intelligent tutoring systems and personalized feedback mechanisms. Yet alongside these remarkable capabilities come profound questions about the nature of authorship, the foundations of academic integrity, equitable access to technological advantages, and the future of scholarly labor and expertise.

This technological inflection point demands not only practical adaptation but also deep reflection on the values and purposes that animate academic work. As generative AI increasingly permeates every aspect of scholarly practice—from the germination of research questions to the final stages of publication and dissemination—we must collectively determine how these tools can best serve the foundational mission of academia: the advancement of human knowledge and understanding through rigorous, creative, and ethical inquiry.

Central to this evolution is the emergence of collaborative AI—systems designed not to replace human scholars but to work alongside them as intellectual partners. These collaborative frameworks represent a fundamental shift from viewing AI as merely automated tools toward understanding them as participatory agents in knowledge creation. Through sophisticated interfaces that facilitate real-time interaction, iterative refinement of ideas, and complementary cognitive strengths, collaborative AI systems are reshaping the very nature of academic teamwork. They enable new forms of intellectual partnership where human creativity, contextual understanding, and ethical judgment combine with computational power, pattern recognition, and information processing at scale.

We synthesize the key insights from our exploration of generative AI in academic contexts, offering conclusions that address both the immediate practical implications and the deeper philosophical questions raised by this technological revolution. Our aim is not to provide definitive answers— indeed, many crucial questions remain open as these technologies continue their rapid evolution—but rather to establish a thoughtful foundation for ongoing dialogue and deliberation within the scholarly community. Through such collective wisdom, we may navigate this transformative moment in ways that harness AI's extraordinary potential while preserving the distinctly human elements that give academic work its ultimate meaning and value.

Paradigm Shift in Research Methodology

Generative AI represents not merely an incremental technological advancement but a fundamental paradigm shift in how academic research is conceptualized and conducted. From the earliest stages of ideation through final dissemination, AI tools are redefining traditional research workflows, accelerating discovery processes, and dramatically augmenting human intellectual capabilities. The technology now enables researchers to process and synthesize vast literature landscapes that would previously have required months or years of human effort, generate novel hypotheses by identifying patterns across seemingly disparate domains, and manage complex, multidimensional datasets with unprecedented efficiency and insight.

This shift is particularly evident in how scholars now approach literature reviews and knowledge synthesis. Where previous generations of researchers were constrained by cognitive limitations in processing the exponentially growing body of academic literature, generative AI tools can now rapidly scan, categorize, and extract key insights from thousands of papers, enabling more comprehensive and nuanced understanding of research domains. Similarly, in data analysis, AI's capacity to identify subtle patterns and correlations is pushing the boundaries of what questions can be meaningfully asked and answered through empirical investigation.

The implications extend beyond mere efficiency gains. As AI becomes increasingly integrated into the research process, we may see fundamental changes in how knowledge is constructed and validated across disciplines, potentially challenging long-established epistemological frameworks and methodological orthodoxies. This suggests not only practical changes in research practice but also deeper philosophical questions about the nature of knowledge production in an age of human-machine collaboration.

Transformation of Academic Writing and Publishing

AI's impact on academic writing and publishing represents a similarly profound transformation of core scholarly practices. While generative AI assistants can help structure, draft, and refine scholarly texts, they also fundamentally raise critical questions about authorship attribution, intellectual contribution, and the very nature of scholarly communication. The evolution of these tools suggests an emerging symbiotic relationship between human creativity and machine capability that may ultimately redefine what it means to be an author in academic contexts.

The ability of AI systems to generate coherent, well-structured academic prose raises important questions about the skills that will be valued in future scholars. If the mechanical aspects of writing can be increasingly automated, scholarly distinction may increasingly depend on conceptual innovation, theoretical insight, and creative synthesis rather than traditional writing prowess. This shift may particularly impact disciplinary traditions where specific writing styles and rhetorical conventions have historically served as markers of academic identity and belonging.

Additionally, AI tools are reshaping the publishing landscape itself, from automated citation management to sophisticated plagiarism detection to AI-assisted peer review systems. These developments suggest a future where the entire publication ecosystem is increasingly mediated by AI technologies, potentially addressing long-standing inefficiencies while also introducing new complexities and challenges to traditional academic gatekeeping functions.

ETHICAL IMPERATIVES AND GOVERNANCE CHALLENGES

The ethical dimensions of AI adoption in academia cannot be overstated and demand urgent, sustained attention from the scholarly community. As these technologies proliferate across institutions, individual scholars, administrators, and policymakers must grapple with increasingly complex questions surrounding data protection, privacy, intellectual property rights, algorithmic bias, and academic integrity. Developing robust ethical frameworks and governance mechanisms will be essential for responsible AI integration that aligns with core academic values.

Particularly concerning are questions of equity and access. If advanced AI tools remain primarily available to well-resourced institutions and scholars, they risk exacerbating existing inequalities in knowledge production and academic influence. Similarly, the environmental impacts of training and deploying large language models and other AI systems raise questions about sustainability and responsibility in research infrastructure.

Academic integrity concerns are equally pressing. As AI-generated text becomes increasingly sophisticated and difficult to distinguish from human writing, traditional notions of plagiarism and assessment of student learning require fundamental reconsideration. Institutions must develop new approaches to evaluating scholarly contribution and student achievement that acknowledge the reality of AI assistance while preserving meaningful standards of intellectual honesty and rigor.

Furthermore, the reliance on AI systems trained primarily on Western academic literature risks reinforcing existing biases in knowledge production and marginalizing non-Western intellectual traditions and epistemologies. Addressing these concerns requires not only technical solutions but also deeper engagement with questions of whose knowledge counts and how diverse intellectual traditions can be meaningfully represented in AI-augmented scholarship.

FUTURE TRAJECTORIES AND ACADEMIC EVOLUTION

The trajectory of AI development strongly suggests its influence in academia will only deepen and expand in coming years. As highlighted in the book's exploration of future trends, we stand at the beginning of a transformative period that will likely redefine scholarly practice across disciplines in ways both anticipated and unforeseen. Academics who develop fluency with these technologies may gain significant advantages in research productivity, impact, and influence, while those who resist adoption risk marginalization in increasingly competitive academic environments.

The integration of multimodal AI systems capable of working across text, images, code, and other data types promises particularly profound changes to interdisciplinary research. These tools may enable new forms of knowledge synthesis that transcend traditional disciplinary boundaries and methodological divides, potentially catalyzing breakthroughs in complex problem domains from climate change to public health.

Emerging applications of generative AI in educational contexts similarly suggest far-reaching changes to teaching practices and student learning experiences. From personalized learning pathways to sophisticated simulation environments, these technologies may transform how disciplinary knowledge and research skills are transmitted to new generations of scholars, with significant implications for curriculum design, pedagogical approaches, and educational assessment.

Furthermore, the accelerating pace of AI development itself poses challenges for academic governance structures and policies, which typically evolve much more slowly than the technologies they seek to regulate. This temporal mismatch suggests the need for more adaptive, principles-based approaches to academic technology governance that can respond to rapidly changing capabilities while maintaining core institutional values.

THOUGHTFUL ENGAGEMENT AND COMMUNITY RESPONSIBILITY

This technological revolution demands thoughtful engagement rather than uncritical adoption or wholesale rejection. The academic community must participate actively and critically in shaping how AI tools evolve and integrate into scholarly practice, ensuring they enhance rather than undermine the core values of academic inquiry: rigor, transparency, integrity, and the advancement of human knowledge.

Particularly important is preserving space for the distinctive forms of human creativity, insight, and judgment that remain beyond AI capabilities. While embracing the efficiencies and new possibilities that AI tools offer, scholars must maintain critical awareness of their limitations and biases, using them as supplements to rather than replacements for human intellectual work.

Institutional responses will be crucial in navigating this transition. Universities, research funders, and scholarly societies must develop thoughtful policies that encourage responsible innovation while safeguarding academic values and addressing ethical concerns. This includes investing in AI literacy for faculty and students, creating appropriate governance structures, and actively participating in broader societal conversations about AI regulation and development.

Ultimately, how generative AI reshapes academia will depend not on technological determinism but on the collective choices of the scholarly community. By approaching these technologies with both openness to their transformative potential and critical awareness of their limitations and risks, academia can harness AI as a powerful tool for advancing human knowledge while preserving the essential human elements of intellectual inquiry.

INDEX

© The Author(s), under exclusive license to Springer Nature Switzerland AG 2025
E. Haber et al., *Using AI in Academic Writing and Research*,
https://doi.org/10.1007/978-3-031-91705-9

GPSR Compliance
The European Union's (EU) General Product Safety Regulation (GPSR) is a set
of rules that requires consumer products to be safe and our obligations to
ensure this.

If you have any concerns about our products, you can contact us on

ProductSafety@springernature.com

In case Publisher is established outside the EU, the EU authorized
representative is:

Springer Nature Customer Service Center GmbH
Europaplatz 3
69115 Heidelberg, Germany